The
Stiletto
Woman

RECLAIMING PERSONAL
EMPOWERMENT

MARISA FERRARO

First Published 2017 by Marisa Ferraro

Published with Ocean Reeve Publishing.

Copyright © Marisa Ferraro 2017

Design by: Ocean Reeve Publishing

Printed and Bound by: Ocean Reeve Publishing

National Library of Australia Cataloguing-in-Publication entry : (paperback) Creator:

Ferraro, Marisa, author.

Title: The Stiletto Woman / Marisa Ferraro.

ISBN: 9781925680072 (paperback)

            9781925680089 (ebook)

Subjects: Dating (Social customs)
            Mate selection.
            Single women.

*Reference
3 Quotes provided by Teymara Antonio Wright
Copright © Teymara Antonio Wright 2011
Wholistic Transformational Therapist, Insight Consultant and Motivational Speaker
www.teymara.com
email: theoffice@teymarainc.com

Ocean
REEVE
PUBLISHING

Contents

*"The Course of
True Love
Never Did Run Smooth."*

– WILLIAM SHAKESPEARE

Chapter 1

Putting the 'Power' in Empowerment

It may have once been said that women are the weaker sex, yet this perception has dramatically changed. Amen. To be a fly on the wall when God created a wo-man. I wonder what he was thinking as he used his Michael Angelo-like powers to make the perfect accompaniment to a man. Hmm?

The fabulous creatures that are women have become part of a revolution. A statement. Over time we have become the stronger sex, the empowered one. Not, however, without blood, sweat and tears. It has taken a long time for the very essence of what a woman is and what she represents to be considered, understood and accepted. Establishing their roles and finding their voice, their path and what they truly want out of life has been no easy feat. Yet women all over the world have achieved it in their own lives and we have much to celebrate.

We have all heard that women are biologically wired to be the nurturer, caretaker and housekeeper. In previous times, foreign to us now, they would look after the children, make sure the home was in order and make dinner for their hunter-gatherer husbands who had been out all day working to provide for and to protect the family. This became the family nucleus for thousands of years. It just was.

Then slowly but surely, like the peeling layers of an onion, the role of women evolved. They engaged in gainful employment and excelled in professional roles. Women returned to work after having babies. They became managers, leaders and entrepreneurs, making money while still caring for their children and their homes. Suddenly women became superwomen. A true force of nature.

Can we do it all? Can we have it all?

Some still struggle with this conundrum today. Juggling has become something that some women feel they are either good at or not, yet is a part of life that must be dealt with. Happily, the persistent forward momentum of feminism has made women what they are today. Women have become more efficient, educated, encouraged and empowered than ever before. The evolution of the 'weaker' sex has been positive, even though somewhat difficult.

We can have it all if we really want to and strive to achieve it. Freedom should be applauded and embraced. It is because of this cultural shift that women have become more self-reliant, resilient and strong. If something doesn't work, we change it, learn from it and better ourselves for it. However, sometimes along the way we still face challenges.

In particular, consider the dating world. Ah yes, the D word. Some of us love to hate it. Just the D word itself can conjure up memories. Dates gone great, dates gone wrong, dates gone great then really wrong. You name it. At some stage, we have all been there and done that.

We may feel empowered in other areas of our lives but not when it comes to dating and men. Why is it that in some situations we feel empowered, assertive and strong, but when it comes to dating a guy we like, all of a sudden our empowerment is gone with the wind? Why is it as soon as they touch a certain chord, we melt and turn to jelly?

First, let's understand the word 'empowerment'.

Empowerment means to become stronger and more confident – to claim your rights and take control of your own life.

When you feel good about yourself, who you are and what you are doing, empowerment feels natural. You feel secure in yourself, what you want and don't want, what you will accept and not accept. You prioritise your needs. With that being said, empowerment is something we incorporate into our everyday life – home, work, relationships and the roller coaster world of dating. Sometimes it's great. Other times, it's crazy.

Crazy. Stupid. Love.

Love, the holy grail that so many men and women strive to attain, can turn men and women into crazy people. Or at the very least make us do crazy things. Things we'd never do in any other situation. It can be 'stupid' in the sense that it makes you feel all kinds of unexplainable feelings, diluting your sense of control. Just that whiff in the air that maybe, just maybe, this person could be the one—it can sweep you off your feet and throw your mind into a tizzy. Edgar Allen Poe once wrote, "I was never insane except when upon occasion love touched my heart." Love can be a kind of temporary insanity that blinds your ability to see yourself and your lover aright.

In a dating situation, you meet someone for the first time, and in seconds you size the person up. How they speak, how they present themselves and how they treat others all create a distinct impression in such a brief moment. All of these factors play a big role in such a brief moment. Are they flirty or funny? Are they dismissive or a little cold towards you? Are you attracted to one another? Those initial pivotal moments could dictate how the entire relationship will go and for how long.

You could say the nose is the organ in question during these potentially crucial moments. From the moment you shake hands, both of you can pick up on the other's pheromones, chemicals secreted through perspiration. These scents send signals to the endocrine system, arousing emotions, behaviours, sexual desires and sex hormones. That's why when someone says, "There was chemistry between us," they are actually not wrong. It is chemistry at work. You may not know this in the moment. But inside, it's activation central. Perfume and after-shave only heighten this sensation. Our sensory department has a lot to do with making or breaking our initial impressions of someone. We must pay respect to our humble nose.

So how does one stay empowered in the moment?

Try to stay in control of your thoughts. The last thing you want is to lose your train of thought and lose the moment. Save the self-reflection for later. Debrief at home. Stay focused and intrigued. You don't know what this person is going to bring into your life and teach you. Whether it's for a fleeting moment or more. Remember what you believe in and your values. If you are about to lose your grip and start to think negatively about the date or initial encounter, remember what you have to gain and what you already have. You want to project your own self-confidence.

The great thing about meeting someone face-to-face is that it gives you visual and auditory cues. You can see their whole composition when they are in front of you and you can hear them too. That makes it a lot easier to know how you feel about a person and to decide whether they are right for you.

Stay in the right frame of mind. If you are angry about something or someone and it is playing on your mind, even if you are out having a drink to unwind and take a load off, it is still there. This can impact how you project yourself to others without you even realising it. If you aren't in the mood and you get approached by a man, it won't be long before that person will be able to tell that your heart's not in it, as the conversation won't be inspiring to either of you.

Negative projection is *dis*empowering.

Your delivery when you speak to someone – even in your body language – has the power to make or break the moment. Are you slouching? Are your shoulders low? Are you smiling or frowning? Are you speaking politely or just giving curt one-word responses? These elements are crucial as they all determine whether your state is empowering or disempowering. There is nothing more wonderful than cheeky banter and flirtation. If it starts off well, then continue. Enjoy the moment and continue on. Don't get so hooked on voices and thoughts of how you think it should be. Be in the flow and in the present. That way there is nothing to be nervous about – you are laughing, you are talking and you are seeing where and if this mild flirtation can go somewhere. You are in control of you. You can continue the conversation or end it depending on how you feel in the space you are in. Just having that control and awareness is empowering.

"Be Happy —
It's Contagious."

Chapter 2
Empowerment in Dating

The dating world can be fun, crazy, frustrating and ever elusive. This is why you have moments of bliss and moments of wanting to bang your head against the wall – or even give up altogether. In those moments, it is important to take a breath and look within yourself. Think about your goals and aspirations. What motivates you? What do you love? What inspires you and makes you feel good? Don't get so caught up in the hype of it all and the 'why' you haven't connected with someone yet.

To lift your mood and give you back that sense of empowerment, start by giving back to yourself. Give to you. Why wait for someone else to give to you? The biggest and most important relationship you will ever have is with yourself – so spoil yourself. If art is what you love, spend time in a gallery or take art classes on the weekends. Buy yourself a nice bunch of flowers for the kitchen. Get a facial. Go for a walk along the beach. Give yourself that feeling, that buzz. Bring that energy of frustration and disappointment to a close by focusing in on yourself – the person you are and the great things about you. This is empowering as you are turning the negative back into a positive with just a few key thoughts and questions.

What do you want? What are five things you are grateful for? What do you love about yourself? What are your favourite things to when you have the time? Remember to ask yourself these when the frustration and stress of dating woes start to appear. When you reflect on what you're happy about and grateful for in your life then a few bad dates seem so trivial in the grand scheme of things.

To extend this positive outlook into your romance, think of dating as fun, even the not-so-great date. After all, if nothing else, it can be a funny story to tell your friends! Simply giving it a go and putting yourself out there is a great step in itself. You're opening the door to opportunity, in whatever form it comes. Even when disappointments and failed attempts seem to besiege you, never falter. Stay empowered. Rise above and beyond the negative energy that doesn't make you feel good and elevate yourself to the energy that does. You'll be surprised to discover that you can almost always find a positive in a negative.

Consider, for example, a relationship that did not work out well or even ended badly. While there seemingly may have been no lesson in this painful episode, when you look at it differently, you can claim your empowerment back. Instead of seeing the situation as bad or thinking things like, *He hurt me. He didn't listen. I was never a priority*, shift your perspective. Nothing can happen to you that you don't *allow* to happen. You are a participant in every situation as well. In this example, ask yourself some questions: Did you communicate to him that you didn't feel like a priority or felt unimportant to him? Did you talk about it or were you angry and abrupt? Did you listen to him? Did you ever think that you hurt him too? Maybe it was something that was said or wasn't said. Perhaps there is no one to blame – you were just two personalities that didn't fit.

Whatever the situation, find your empowerment by asking the right questions in retrospect in order to see it from another vantage point. This type of self-reflection will, in most cases, help you to find a positive in a negative. Having gone through a bunch of dates or maybe a short-term relationship, what did it teach you? Maybe you learned to compromise better or to be more patient. Perhaps you learned empathy and you allowed yourself to be vulnerable. You may have learned the balance between personal space and together space. You may have learned more about yourself – what you like, what you don't like, what you can tolerate, what you will accept and how to forgive.

There is no such thing as a coincidence. See each situation as a moment in time and a gift. Even if it is painful. There are so many lessons that are indirectly taught from experiences. Exes can actually teach us and strengthen us. Even the most difficult and annoying ones. From each experience, there is growth. In every relationship, there is room for change, and 'failed' relationships offer a wealth of lessons to learn as you grow. Each person and dating relationship is a teacher. You attract what you need when you need it. It's part of evolving as a being. So keep the faith always. Even in the most emotionally difficult times. Be open to experiences. Be open to love. Be open to life.

All of these ideas help to contribute to our personal empowerment. We can cultivate this positive mindset more and more as we live our daily lives and see what scenarios we find ourselves in – particularly in the world of dating. The process of dating can be often frustrating and difficult. If we break through the misconception that it's 'hard work' and nothing but going from one bad date to another, and if we don't place too much pressure on ourselves, it can be a fun experience.

It all comes down to your core feeling. When you are in a low mood, you may slouch, walk slower, keep your head and face down. You won't have a smile or lit eyes. However, when you are empowered within yourself, you feel good, both emotionally and physically. Even your posture is upright – you 'walk the talk'. You may not notice it, but it absolutely projects when you are out and about. When you are at your optimum feeling, your facial expressions and body language project it. That's what empowerment does.

Empowerment comes when you are being your best self. It goes hand in hand with how you value yourself and knowing what you are deserving and worthy of. The more worthy you feel, the less likely you are to put up with situations – whether professionally or personally – that bring you down or make you feel less than valuable. You become attuned to your feelings, enabling you to recognise when a situation is wrong for you and how to take action to either change it, adjust your feelings towards it or remove yourself from the situation completely. The lower your level of power and self-esteem, the more you are likely to put up with negative situations or partners.

If a situation or experience isn't bringing out your best self and is making you think or behave in ways that are *dis*empowering, then you are doing a *dis*service to yourself to allow it to continue. As challenging as it may be, taking the step toward self-love and true happiness within will ultimately make you empowered and stronger.

Sometimes when we're dating someone, we might talk ourselves into accepting an unhealthy relationship. You tell yourself that there is nothing you can do about it, so you continue on and let it drag you down and engulf you. But here's the thing. There is no empowerment in this scenario. Find a way to communicate how you feel. Express yourself and what you believe in. The other person involved isn't going to know if you don't tell them. It takes courage to do it – to put yourself out there and be assertive. But it does your aura a world of good if you do. Being true and honest with yourself is the most empowering step you can take. After you do it once, it will serve as a stepping stone for you to remain in that state for other moments when relationships go wrong.

Put simply: inner core values + worth = empowerment.

The more you embrace your own worth, the better you will feel and the more you will attract better situations. Even a better man. It is not always easy. You may not feel like heroine twenty-four hours of the day, every single day. There will be days where all you will want is your pyjamas and a box of chocolates, watching *Pretty Woman* on the couch. Allow yourself that from time to time, of course, but don't let it get a hold of you and your life. Don't lose your momentum altogether. Enjoy those insular moments when you need to, but make sure you get up, remember your worthiness and uniqueness and get moving. As Thomas S. Monson wrote, "If you want to give light to others, you have to glow yourself."

"It's When
You are at Your
Happiest that the
Magic Happens."

Chapter 3

The Stiletto and the Woman

The stiletto: a classic and universal symbol of finding true love, finding yourself and finding the path you want for yourself. Something magical happens – not only your self-esteem but to your sense of being as a woman – when your feet slip into a pair of heels. To many, the stiletto is the 'IT' factor of the entire ensemble, an effect that transcends mere wardrobe completion.

Every little girl knows that when Cinderella lost her stiletto, the prince not only found the shoe, he found *his princess* at the same time. Of course this is a fairy tale. But for many women, wearing stilettos makes them feel like a princess. With or without a prince.

Ah, yes! This fabulous accoutrement designed for women's feet symbolises love, sex and power – all while creating an absolutely stunning visual effect. A staple possession worn by women the world over, stilettos can make the ultimate statement and have quite an effect on how we feel. Like magic, once we are dressed and finally slip into our shoes before walking out the door, they transform our whole posture and demeanour. They can make us feel complete – ready to conquer the world. That extra bit of height lifts us not just physically – making us feel more attractive – but also emotionally, boosting our confidence and making us feel more powerful.

Subconsciously or not, we feel the power and, as such, we allocate time with a dedicated passion to go out and buy shoes. Footwear shopping goes beyond ordinary retail therapy. It's the euphoric rush of giving to *ourselves*, not just our wardrobes, and feeding our inner confidence. And who better to spoil you and feed your inner confidence than *you*?

As feet aren't at eye level, they can potentially be the last thing noticed in human-to-human contact. This is where sophisticated shoe designers come in. Artists such as Christian Louboutin, Manolo Blahnik, Giuseppe Zanotti and Versace are creative geniuses who understand the power of an elegant pair of heels as the ultimate symbol of femininity – and female empowerment.

But how can this be? Any girl who's donned a pair of four-inch pumps for an evening of fun knows how quickly these sexy accessories can turn into instruments of torture. They can pinch, scrape and squeeze tiny toes to within an inch of their little lives and – while they lift you a few precious centimetres about the crowd – have you feeling as though you're teetering on the brink of falling all night while you clutch shakily at your dirty martini. Beauty is pain, as they say. You may have to deal with blisters while you wear flats for three days just to recover. But is it worth it? Absolutely. It isn't so much about the pain. It's about the feeling. As women, we want to feel like a goddess. The stiletto does that to a woman.

Ever since the lipstick feminist movement set out to rework the dichotomy of sexual power and feminist ideals in order to celebrate femininity and sexuality, popular culture strutted the stiletto back into the limelight in shows such as *Sex and the City*. Through this movement, the power of the pump has inverted a symbol of female sexual submission into an icon of women's sexual *authority*, in sync with lipstick feminist ideals. The stilettoed woman has become a modern-day hunter who's reclaimed her personal empowerment. The blade of the stiletto itself has become a phallic extension of the female leg that epitomises her sexual potency in a patriarchal world.

The stiletto elongates the female form and invites a tantalising mix of sexuality and mental calisthenics. A woman precariously tries to maintain her balance, reclaim her power and free herself from a sense of male dominance. Yes, it's still a sex symbol. But by embracing it, women *own* their sexual power – not men. The stiletto has the ability to scream, *Damn, this girl means business!* which can be an extension of her control in any situation.

Take, for instance, the corporate world. Women in the office environment wear formal attire such as a tailored suit, and complemented with the stiletto, the look emanates authority, class and strength. The heel lengthens the leg, making you look taller, and as your posture grows more erect, you command people's attention. The stiletto in the corporate world has long been associated with confidence and power.

The connection between a woman and her heels is a powerful one, especially after the emotional blow of a breakup. So much more than a fashion accessory, it can be an extension of her search for reclaiming her confidence and personal power. It's like Prozac for the feet. It's the much-needed endorphin rush after an emotional avalanche has brought you to your knees. It's that quest to bring your sense of self and your sense of being a woman back together again after feeling like a 7-inch heel has pierced your heart. Like any relationship, the connection a woman has with her heels involves investment, commitment and sacrifice. Yet the payoffs are huge.

Stilettos for women are like prestige cars for men. They are the ultimate statement. They are what we dream about, and we make time and effort for them. Shoe shopping is not only retail therapy, it's giving yourself the gift of empowerment. And you should feel good about doing this. If you can't give to yourself, who else will do it?

"*Power is Something You Harness Within. Only You Can Give it to You.*"

Chapter 4
The End of Human Connection

The dating world has changed quite a bit over the last couple of decades. We are now texting, MMSing and Instagramming each other. It seems everyone knows that you had blueberries for breakfast and you were at the theatre on the weekend. You don't have to call and tell your friend that news – she's already seen it on Facebook.

You can have a cyber relationship in an instant. Twenty years ago, no one would have dreamed that the Internet would become so integral to dating that people feel obliged to go on a computer to meet a potential date, yet the dawn of the new millennium has thrust us into the digital age – dates and all. We swipe left or right, making swift judgements on photos and choosing whether we will reply or not. It has also become easier than ever to flake out on a relationship by simply fading into the digital void of non-response. Or dump someone via the most impersonal, destructive and dismissive way possible: text message.

Basic respect has been lost in translation – or, to be more specific, lost in cyber translation. In this new way of communicating, have we forgotten genuine honest-to-goodness face-to-face interactions? Pre-millennium, a boy used to drive to his girlfriend's house to see her – there was no other way. It required effort to make a connection. Now you can do almost anything online or on the phone. The effort is diminished and that early human connection in the foundations of a relationship is diluting. If a guy wants a visual, he can get it on the phone or FaceTime – even before you've met! So little effort is required. Additionally, with hundreds of emojis to depict how you feel, it seems people no longer endeavour to dig deep into their feelings to try to express themselves. You can just send a funny symbol. You can practically tell an entire story in symbols. Through the two-dimensional nature of text messages, relationships can get compromised and questioned, comments can get taken out of context and arguments can be ignited via the misinterpretation of words on a screen. Rather than picking up the phone to engage with someone by listening to their words and tone of voice, messaging has become the new norm.

We all do it and we all justify it. Life is hectic. Work hours are long. Household and family chores seem never-ending. Texting can save time and is quick and easy. But when did it *replace* face-to-face human connection? Texting is impersonal and often misconstrued. Messages are misread and taken out of context, particularly when you don't know the sender's personality yet, all because the human connection of seeing and hearing was not present. It has become common for guys to ask girls out via texting. Where is the romance in that? Where is the connection? It's so cold, so stale. Women, however, respond in kind, so it becomes the way to communicate.

If you let the man know that you prefer to converse with people, then maybe he will lift his game and pick up the phone.

But your partner won't know if you don't tell him. Be open and communicate how you feel and what you want.

In order to gain some empowerment in this area, explain to your man of interest that speaking over the phone or face-to-face is how you'd prefer to interact. That way you know where you stand on this matter and so will he. Set the standard early and be clear. Maintain your boundaries. You may find he will start to respect you for telling him how you feel.

If he is a serial texter, then he may not be respecting you and your feelings about communicating. He may lack the basic skills of social communication. Of course, things like 'I'll be a little late' or 'See you at 6' are just quick notes and totally fine, and sometimes it's not possible or necessary to call. But to talk more deeply and really get to know someone, speaking on the phone or in person is the best way to go. It's the only way to build up some banter and see how it develops. When you have auditory (and visual) cues, it is much easier to decipher a person, as a lot of subconscious body language and audio inflections are also communicated. The delivery, the posture, the mannerisms, the sound of the voice – all of these things are pivotal in ascertaining what the person is saying, where the conversation is going and what the person is like.

Communication is the most important element in any relationship. The overuse of digital communication is making us lose that personal touch, that intimate way of connecting. You don't even have to go see your girlfriend or boyfriend now as you can FaceTime them. If you want to see your girlfriend or boyfriend naked, you can ask for pictures. While this may be a fun and exciting thing to do for some, isn't the real thing better?

Where is the human connection, the intimacy and the feeling? We are creatures designed to feel. Wouldn't it be more beautiful on an intimate level to experience these things on a one-on-one personal level? You can't fall in love via text message. When it comes to love, the good old-fashioned way works best.

Etiquette has flown out the window in a lot of instances. Where is the courtship in asking someone out on a text? If a man wants to see you, he should call you to make arrangements, not have a ten-minute text session with you. Wouldn't it just be easier on the phone? Alas, not for some. This habit is hard to break. But it's the lazier approach. Men think this behaviour is acceptable and we have, perhaps inadvertently, allowed it to happen. It has become second nature. We do it without realising it. The over-reliance on texting has allowed some people to let their communication skills to go a little rusty – if they ever had them in the first place. Have we women brought in the goal posts and dropped our standards? Perhaps. But what you can know for sure is that if you allow constant texting to be your gateway of communication, then he will assume it's okay and will keep doing it.

Reclaim your power through human contact, not digital interaction. There is value to be found in building relationships the way it used to be done. There is a level of decorum involved with face-to-face communication. It now has become too easy to hit 'delete' and walk away when conflict enters the relationship. Even if things aren't working out and the end of a relationship is nigh, isn't it more respectable to meet up and talk in person rather than dumping him or her with a text, 'delete' button or ignoring them? Ghosting. The new way to avoid facing up to an ending. A cowardly approach to ending it with someone without thought or explanation. Easy, yes. Respectable? No. But it has happened to many, for sure.

What should you do when you have been ghosted? When you have been ghosted, it is important to not blame yourself and to keep the negative self-talk to a minimum. Now, that's easier said than done. But if you are treating your partner with honesty and respect and all of a sudden it seems like your texts and calls are being ignored, then it's most likely that the unfriendly ghost has come your way. Not your fault. It's just that the person does not have enough consideration for your feelings to tell you the truth and set you free in a respectable way. Sometimes the best thing to do is accept that that person wasn't meant for you. If they can't respect you enough to face you, then why would you want them anyway? Cut them loose. Even if it hurts.

Relationships are harder now because conversations have devolved into texting, arguments are left to phone calls, feelings get expressed in subliminal messages, sex is easy, the word 'love' is used out of context, insecurities become a way of thinking, getting jealous becomes a habit, trust is hard to come by, being hurt is natural and leaving seems like the only option.

It seems that for whatever reason, mobile phones have diminished our ability to be personal and respectful in the many situations we find ourselves in. Keep your empowerment by communicating how you want to be spoken to and treated. That way, he will know how to behave towards you.

Empower yourself to use the correct form of communica-tion when necessary. Not only are you setting an example but you will gain more clarity and understanding. You may also be more respected for your level of communication and connection to the people you're dealing with, which applies to both dating and human relationships in general. Communication is key and so is empowerment – as you may have noticed, they are interrelated.

In a working environment, if you want a raise or promotion, or to do well in your current project because you want to gain more credibility, you put in additional time and effort. You don't cut corners. You do your due diligence. You prove to your boss that you are worthy. Your lines of communication are clear and concise.

Why should dating be any different?

Why cut corners and do an average job and not communicate clearly as to what you want and what you are doing? Why should a man get away with being half-assed or lazy? A man should show you why he is worth your time and energy. Let him show you why you should respond to his affections. It isn't always in what a man says; it's what he *does*. Be the observer. If you give in early, you will lose your sense of empowerment. Is he a texter ninety percent of the time? Or is he making time to speak to you? Is he making the effort to see you? Is he interesting in what you say when you do speak? Does he value your time? Or does he keep you guessing or hanging? These subtle hints early on are good indicators of how he will treat you in the future.

You hold the power. You call the shots. You have the power to say yes or no. And only you know how *you* feel. Friends can only do so much and give their opinions based on their own experiences. So go with your gut instincts. If his style of communication is bothering you, then tell him about it and be clear. If he changes his behaviour for the better, then that suggests that he respects your thoughts and is willing to take responsibility for his own actions.

If not, he may not be in the right space or he may not be the right person for you. If he is not respecting your time, making an effort or being true to his word, chances are you should drop him like a hot potato. Empower yourself and move on. Cut the ties early. You are far too important to waste your time on someone who doesn't respect you. Give yourself space and time to attract a real gentleman.

*"Body Language
Speaks Volumes."*

Chapter 5
All about Eve

Now let's talk about Adam and Eve. Not the ones in the garden, but the ones from which all human life extends. The mitochondrial Eve is the most recent ancestor of all current living humans. To put it simply, she is the 'mother' of all mothers. Our matriarch. The male counterpart is Adam, of course. Or in palaeontology talk, Y-Chromosomal Adam. He is the leader of all male homo sapiens. The term 'mitochondrial Eve' alludes to the biblical Eve. For the last 2000 years or so, Eve has represented the fundamental character and identity of all women. Through her words and actions, the true nature of women was revealed. Eve, to many historians, philosophers and theologians, represents everything about a woman a man should guard against. In both form and symbol, Eve is woman, and because of her, the prevalent belief in the West has been that all women are by nature disobedient, guileless, weak-willed, prone to temptation and evil, disloyal, untrustworthy, deceitful, seductive and motivated in their thoughts and behaviour purely by self-interest.

No matter what women might achieve in the world, the message given from these biblical interpretations warn men not to trust women, and women not to trust themselves or each other. Whoever she might be and whatever her accomplishments, no woman can escape being identified with Eve and the suggestion that there is a little bit of Eve inside of her. And biologically speaking, that is true. Every woman does have a little of the mitochondrial Eve inside her very cells. No wonder men have read women all wrong. No wonder love is a battlefield and filled with confusion, commitment-phobes and men who love 'em and leave 'em.

But time has evolved and women have too. Dear Adams of the homo sapiens world, there is nothing to be confused about. You are the hunter and gatherers of the program. So hunt and gather. It's really simple. It may actually be fun. Isn't it better that women come with many facets of being? Wouldn't you get bored if she was one-dimensional?

True, Eve took it upon herself to bite an apple. This fruit is a symbol of temptation and ultimately sin. How can eating the apple have been a sin when Adam and Eve were made to spread their genes and DNA as much as possible? Wasn't procreation the main agenda?

Procreation, some would say, is life as we know it. The biblical theory of giving into temptation is actually something that is in our biology to do. Forbidden? I think not. Could 'giving into temptation' perhaps be a more diplomatic way of saying that we have actually come on this earth as man and woman to breed? Yet this apple that Eve took it upon herself to eat was somehow misconstrued and seen as the ultimate sin. In the biblical sense, it actually wasn't. What was she supposed to do with Adam? Exchange pleasantries and sip a cup of tea? The

Bible never connects eating the apple with sex. If anything, God made man and woman as he did to enjoy each other (including sexually) and encouraged them to do so (one of the books of the Bible is about that, Song of Songs) and told them to do so ("be fruitful and multiply…"). But he also told them they could eat of any tree in all of the garden except this one tree, the Tree of the Knowledge of Good and Evil. But they thought that if they broke the one rule he gave them, that they could be like God (when they already were… since he made them in his image), so they broke that one rule and came to know evil, for sure. Sex wasn't forbidden between them, it was encouraged. How one simple day on the green got so confusing and become the basis on which man and woman relations conform is beyond me.

Sex is wonderful and we all can enjoy it. Oxytocin, or the big 'O', is a fancy medical term for the feel-good cuddle hormone, widely referred to as the 'love hormone'. When we are intimate, we release it. Lots of it. The more 'cake' we get the more of this magnificent chemical engulfs us. Suddenly we are having the best sex of our lives and we want him more and more (our inner dialogue begins: *He must really like me a lot. He stays with me and is so cute and cuddly. He must be The One*). Metaphorically, this type of 'logic' comes from the heart, not the brain. Scientifically, these thoughts are influenced by our hormone releases and not through the unadulterated use of the prefrontal cortex.

Our logic flies out the window during this intense intimate period of hormonal release. It feels like we are at a buffet where we can't get enough. This man can suddenly do no wrong. He ticks all the boxes. Any little annoying habit that may surface just fades into the background because he is gorgeous and a dynamite in bed.

The problem is, while oxytocin makes you feel good, it also to some degree impairs judgement, which in turn can result in women losing power in those crucial early days. The power we thought we had goes out the window the moment we reach our peak level. We are consumed. Not only do we release our inhibitions, but we release many other things, it seems. 'Adam', in this case, is king. He does what he wants to do and does it well. So well in fact, that he can do that again and again. Eve wants him and needs him and will do anything for him. She makes herself totally available to him. She brings him his coffee, gets him lunch, bakes him his favourite cake and offers to pick up his dry cleaning. The list goes on. Adam knows this and loves the attention and pandering. He knows he can say or do anything and she will continue to be available. She often accepts this treatment blindly, even if some elements of the relationship seem wrong or out of order because he is The One. Adam can get his hands on her anytime he wants, as Eve keeps herself open and available to him. Eve wants Adam and will do anything to keep him.

This is where life gets interesting. Or crazy, depending on the pair. But where do you draw the line between biology and core values? Can't a woman have both? We definitely can. It isn't so much about sexual liberty and expression as such but being true to yourself, honouring your feelings and decisions and having control of all aspects of your being.

Lets call the symbol of fertility and the essence of where all life begins as 'The Chalice Cup'. It is the holy grail of a man's wants and needs. It is what he craves. Some would say that sex for men is like oxygen for the lungs. You have to have it and can't live very long without it. Now what could be the difference between holding back a little as opposed to giving in easily and freely? A few things could occur.

By keeping the lid on the cup, it can do wonders for your self-esteem and self-worth. Moreover, it keeps him in a place of wanting to be with you more. Remember, men love being the hunter. It's in their genetic code to do so. So let him. Let him prove to you why he is worthy. Working for it provides a much more satisfying feeling to a man's sense of masculinity than achieving something that is given so easily and openly.

If the opposite happens and he bails after his sexual advances are rejected, consider it a blessing that he has walked away from you. It's doubtful he was looking for any kind of commitment. Instead, he just wanted some no-strings-attached casual fun. It may seem disappointing at the time, especially if you were really keen on him, but you have to accept he wasn't the man you were looking for. Now you can continue on the path to meeting the right person.

Weeding out the duds is necessary when trying to find someone who will value you and your time. Women have always had the upper hand; we just sometimes forget that when giving into temptation. Stay in the driver's seat. Observe how a man treats a woman who readily gives into temptation and compare her to the ones that don't. It's up to you which kind of woman you want to be and which result you want to have.

When you know when the moment is right and you decide to be intimate with him, separate the act from the hormones.

He's not God because he gave you a climax that resembled Moses parting the Red Sea. He is a man, nothing more and nothing less. Keep your sense of self and stay true to you. That's ultimately the most empowering gift you can give yourself, and when the right man comes along, he will be grateful to have you in his life.

Women do have the upper hand in all areas of a relationship if you really think about it. That most likely drives men crazy. We choose whether or not to accept their advances. We choose whether or not to bite into the apple. We choose to allow certain behaviours from men. We run our own races. As for The Chalice cup, it's your preference on how you want to work it and deal with it that matters. So whether sex is an act driven by biology or something in line with your core values, the decision to have it is entirely yours. Own it and love it. Whatever you do. Darlings, your cup runeth over.

"The Beauty of a Woman Can Not Only Be Seen But Also Felt."

Chapter 6
Persistence is King

Dating and being single can take up a lot of time and energy. You have euphoric highs and some crushing lows. However, when you are actively dating and are open to opportunities, these highs and lows have a lot to do with your attitude and your feelings and perspective. You need to be patient and persist. Particularly through the frustrating dry spells where it seems that nothing is going right and you are only meeting Neanderthals.

If you are in the zone of negative momentum or feeling stuck, then maybe take a break from dating for a while. As with anything, you have to have the right frame of mind and the right attitude to succeed, otherwise the right occasions won't happen as you won't attract them. If you are over the whole dating scene and feeling exhausted, put it on hold for a while. Recharge and be free from the hustle and bustle of it all. Take that energy and concentrate on the things you love and the life you want to lead.

But don't confuse taking a break with giving up. Never give up hope, as all is possible and doable. You must believe and hold unwavering faith that what will be will be and that what is meant for you will come. It will come in the divine time and way that it is meant to. What you need to do is carry on and keep doing what you are doing. It can actually be that simple.

Focusing on yourself for a while is a great way to re-energise and get your empowerment and self-focus back. Use your new energy, focus and power to do things that make you happy and try new things you've always wanted to do but have never gotten around to. It's never too late. Dating hang-ups happen to all of us at some stage or another. Don't let them weigh you down and don't let that be your only focus. Take back those thoughts and make them positive. Bring the power back to you.

It is often when you are in the momentum of living your life and living your passions that you seem to attract the right people and circumstances into your life. If you are in the right headspace emotionally, spiritually and mentally, then it's all a matter of timing. You have the power to make the right choices and take the right steps, which is just as true for career opportunities as it is for relationships. Changing the way you feel about dating is the first step. Be open to different forms of dating, such as online dating or speed dating. You have no way of knowing where or how you'll meet that special someone you click with, so broaden your opportunities. Similarly, there are no wasted experiences. You may meet someone whom you don't quite click with, but they could unlock a blockage inside of you or end up introducing you to new friends or a new romantic prospect.

Never go into a date thinking negative thoughts like, *This is a chore, I'm only doing it because my friends made me and I probably won't like him anyway.* Going into it with negative assumptions will not make you feel good. But being open, excited, curious and optimistic will put you in good spirits and that will show on your date. You may even really hit it off with someone, leading to more dates.

Never write off anything as a waste of time. Instead, think about what that person taught you. Maybe you became clearer on what you do and don't want in a potential partner. Maybe he taught you something new that you didn't know before. Maybe he gave you feelings that you had never felt before and you enjoyed. Each date and everyone you meet when you are out there puts you in a better position as it allows you to further understand more about yourself, what you will tolerate, what you will accept and what you like in a person, as well as what your standards are and what you require from your partner. It becomes like a self- discovering journey. Think of it like practice. To prepare you for the right one.

So even though a date may not have gone as you'd hoped it would, you still stay empowered as you stay true to yourself and your requirements from your date, without giving into negative thinking or discouragement. Don't self-sabotage or give off negative energy. It can be difficult at times but stay focused on you and just recharge. Focus on your beliefs, your values and your goals. Most importantly, focus on all the blessings that are already in your life.

Persist, persist, persist.

You may decide to date in phases. That's perfectly fine! Do what feels right. Every experience will prepare you for the next. See dating, even with all its frustrations, as an opportunity for expansion and growth. You will grow as a woman. Self-love paints your entire world. So love yourself enough to say, *Okay, that didn't go as well as I hoped, but I will learn from it because*

I deserve happiness. Learn from the situation. Nothing is ever a waste of time if what you're gaining is strength, understanding and allowing yourself to rise above and grow from that experience.

Don't accept anything short of amazing.

Balance the negative with a positive. It's like yin and yang. When you focus and attune your thoughts and attitude to the positive, the negative gets smaller and smaller. By choosing empowering thoughts and actions, it diminishes the negative sabotage that goes on in our minds. You may think there is something wrong with you when a relationship turns sour. Empower your thinking by not blaming yourself. Have compassion for yourself, just as you would for a close friend. The right time and space will allow the right person to come along.

Whenever a date or relationship doesn't end well, turn it into a positive by considering all the things you *did* gain from the experience, such as making new friends, going on a holiday to somewhere you'd never been before, having new experiences – even becoming a mother. Always remember that even though something didn't work as you'd hoped, there's always a positive to be found.

As Mary Lou Retton once said, "Optimism is a happiness magnet. If you stay positive, good things and good people will be drawn to you."

"When a Woman Knows Herself, Knows What She Wants and Oozes Confidence — That Is Sexy."

Chapter 7
When All That's Good Goes Bad

When things are going great, being happy seems effortless. You feel like you are floating on air, like all the planets have aligned and nothing can go wrong. It's great when life seems to be running smoothly. So when things do get tough, and they do, when your sweet new relationship starts to sour, how do you turn things around?

Life can be fickle. It can test you, and this also applies to love. When things get difficult or more challenging, it is important to reflect and revise. Look at the situation in its entirety. Consider different perspectives, not just your own. This may assist in clarifying the issue and also in reminding yourself of how you feel and what you want. What are your standards and expectations? Don't let them fall by the wayside. These considerations will empower you to stay focused and strong during times of difficulty. So acknowledge your feelings and your values.

In the early days of dating, if something seems somewhat odd to you or makes you uncomfortable, don't feel obliged to continue. Talk about it if you feel that you need clarity in under-standing a situation or behaviour. But stand firm and stay true to yourself. It may take a few goes to get it right. That's okay. It all serves as a lesson. Every date is different and everyone you meet has a different vibe and energy to them. The important thing is to know whether you are on the same energy path and in sync with each other. Usually you see that on the first date or two. Sometimes it's immediate, which is great! We all love those dates where we hit it off straightaway.

When things are going smoothly in the beginning, remember to keep communication lines open. You don't know what the other person is feeling or what they are thinking, and we run the risk of projecting our own desires onto them. We can be quick to assume things, but making assumptions often fails to give you facts. However, talking about it does. Avoid getting yourself into a state of anxiety or frustration, which minimises your empowerment. Remember assuming is just a thought. Not fact. It is better to talk and find out rather than allowing your mind to go overboard with hypothesizing. You are the driver, you are in control. What you do, how you handle a situation (good or bad) is up to you and your state of being. This may be difficult as you may also dealing with all the internal alchemy. So you are fighting logic, which is what you need, with powerful physical and emotional desires. The butterflies-in-your-stomach feeling.

Say you are getting ready for a date and you're feeling excited about seeing the guy. After putting your outfit together and polishing it off with some nice shoes, you feel good, hopeful and excited. Empowered. You want to show him the best of you. When you feel good about yourself, it is a little easier to navigate a date, whether good or bad. It's a wise idea to keep your expectations under control. Don't expect perfection. As you know, there is no such thing as perfection. One of the greatest poets of all time knew a thing or two about dating when he wrote: "Expectation is the root of all heartache." William Shakespeare had a point. Be open to going with the flow. That way, you can minimise the disappointment when a date isn't stellar. At the very least, you can say to yourself that you gave it a go and tried.

Say the first date went really well and he mentioned at good night that he will touch base and catch up with you soon. True to form, he did call you (brownie points for Mr Date) and you go out again. As it was, you had a great time. You conversed about many things and found you had a number of interests in common. Then, slowly but surely, conflicts surface that seem minor at first but start to unnerve you. Like his unpredictability. He changes plans at the last minute or makes excuses when running late. Perhaps it gets to the point where he can reach you and you are available yet you can never get a hold of him. Or he may say one thing and mean another. All of a sudden, the man you started going out with shows a very different side – one that you were unaware of and weren't prepared for. When a man is in the company of a good woman and he can't prove to her that he will treat her with respect and will be honest with her, then he is not deserving of her time. Giving your time to someone is one of the most valuable things you can give. Particularly in the beginning. Time is an investment. When you are 'into' someone, you invest your time. This is crucial. If the person you are seeing can't respect that, then he is not worthy of you. It shows that you might not be high on his priority list. Upsetting as it is. This is a good indication of what kind of person he is. Sure we all make mistakes, but a mistake and taking someone for granted are two different things.

When the dates go well and then starts to go poorly, remove yourself from the situation and see what happens. He may get in contact with you again or he may not. Either way, you have your answer. Remember your worth and your values. Stay in this vibration so you can attract someone that understands this. As the self-help guru Karen Salmansohn writes, "Sometimes when bad things happen, we learn to appreciate them in a whole new light."

Regardless of what is to come or how it goes, always give yourself credit for trying and stay empowered with the knowledge and certainty that "what's meant for you will not pass you by."

Ask yourself empowering questions. What are the achievements that make me most proud? What do I want for the future? What brings me the most happiness? What do I love about myself? Never get into the state where a string of bad dates and courting woes gives you negative thoughts that make you feel bad about yourself. Be proud of the woman you are and for putting yourself out there. Life throws curve balls, and finding love and lasting connections will surely bring a mixture of pleasure and pain. Getting into the habit of reflecting, thinking positively and being open to opportunity is key. This will assist in a sustained level of empowerment.

It is the journey, not the destination, that is important. See life as it is and have fun with it. So be kind to yourself. Love yourself enough to know that through a difficult situation you become stronger, you get to know your strengths and your weaknesses. You grow, learn and evolve. This is empowering. Own your feelings. You are human and it's okay to make a mistake and to learn from them. It's all a part of life.

" Beauty is an Inside Job."

Chapter 8
Glutton for Punishment

Every experience is different. How boring would it be if everyone was the same and we all experienced the same thing over and over again? Variety is the spice of life, and dating is a mix of the good, the bad, the ugly and the super-fab. It's a mixed game. You never really know what's next.

It's funny how we never really forget a bad experience. It makes for a good laugh over drinks with friends. Everyone has a story. After a not-so-great dating episode, you try to learn from it and say, *I'll never do that again* or *I won't make myself so available next time – he'll have to prove himself first* – and so forth. We kick often ourselves for going back and giving them another chance when we knew deep down we shouldn't have. We listen to that female voice of compassion whispering, *Give him the benefit of the doubt*, yet we end up falling flat on our faces yet again. We sabotage the way we feel because we blame ourselves for opening up and being vulnerable, even when it didn't get us anywhere. But why, against our better judgement, do we go back and repeat the same mistakes? Is it a force of nature built into the female genetic code or just a bad habit? How do we lose our way? We go into a relationship with the right intentions but sometimes find ourselves doing the very things we said we wouldn't do from the last experience.

Are we gluttons for punishment?

Everyone, at some stage, has waited for that phone to ring – or has even taken the proactive approach of calling him to instigate the next date or just to say hello. He may say he will call you back but never does, leaving you filled with disappointment and frustration. Don't give away your empowerment! Just take the situation for what it is and don't get hung up on the fact that it didn't go anywhere. The proof is in the pudding. If he wanted you, nothing would stop him. No ifs, ands or buts. The rest is excuses. If a man says he will take you to dinner or to a movie or for brunch and he does, then he is a man of his word and someone you could potentially build a relationship with.

If he doesn't, he's all talk and probably not all that keen.

Simple.

When you refocus on the various aspects of your life that give you fulfilment, the over-obsessing about a man or date will subside. You won't be as perplexed as to why conflicts arose; you'll realise more that talk is cheap and you will get on with all the other elements of your life that have meaning. You can't force love, even though you may think it's something you truly want. All things flow in divine timing. A man of his word will call and keep calling. A man who flatters his own ego for the night with false promises won't. See the end of this relationship as a good thing – a blessing in disguise – as you don't want to waste time on a bullshit artist. You want, need and deserve someone who is going to be real with you. You will learn a lot about a man by his actions.

Once again:

What's meant for you will not pass you by.

This goes for everything in life. As you learn from experience, empowerment begins to stay with you. There may be moments in which it lays dormant – but it stays within you. We all have it. We just need to nurture it from time to time, especially when the going gets tough.

Think of a banana. There are the hard bananas that need time to ripen, the perfectly ripe bananas and the ones that are too ripe and have spoiled a little inside. We have learned by experience that the hard ones still need to ripen as they are inedible, even though from the outside the colour looks pretty good. It may be ready, but it might not be – despite the fact that you really want the banana now. Deep down you know it isn't ready. If you start to peel the banana anyway, you'll only to discover that you first inkling was right. The banana wasn't as sweet and soft as you'd hoped. You are disappointed that you peeled it as the experience wasn't what you were looking for. You knew this would be the case, yet you still went there in the hope that it would be different. But the banana wasn't ready. Had you waited until it was or picked a softer, yellower banana, then the experience would have been different. With a ripe banana – one that was ready – you would have gotten a sweet and satisfying experience.

Similarly there is the overripe banana. Sometimes you pick it, even though it's too soft and starting to brown, in the hope that it will still be good inside. Yet inside it isn't what you envisioned and it's difficult to find any edible bits, so you really don't get much out of it. Once again you made a hasty decision, ignoring your better judgement. You could see that the overripe banana was out of date and, thus, too sweet and bruised inside. Yet you peeled that banana anyhow and didn't get much from it.

You may have guessed by now, but we're not feel down talking about bananas. The analogy just goes to demonstrate principles that apply to dating. Unfortunately, we sometimes go for someone we thought we wanted, brushing our reasoning and instincts aside, only to find that they weren't the person we hoped they'd be. They might have looked good on the outside. They might have 'fit the profile' of whom you thought you wanted. But the connection wasn't really there.

There is an old saying – if it seems too good to be true, it probably is.

We've all made the mistake of picking the one we thought we wanted rather than the one we know we're better suited to. And – let's be honest – sometimes we can make this mistake a few times over before we learn, even though past pickings have done us wrong. Being a sucker for repeated mistakes in love happens. Perhaps it's a learning experience on some cosmic level and we need to go through it again until we get the message. The important thing is to re-empower yourself after a letdown. Don't let it get you down for too long. You just pick yourself up and move on. You will eventually be lead to the right circumstance, the right time in the right way. Listening to your gut is pivotal. Be focused and aware. Gut instinct is a great way to retain a sense of empowerment. Patience is not only a virtue but a must. It's not always easy but it's necessary when dealing with this thing called love.

Implement your learning from the past sooner rather than later. If you feel that what is going on is similar to a past experience that didn't go well, then remember what you learned and make different choices this time.

It is difficult when things aren't going so great and deep down you know it. Sometimes we are gluttons for punishment, so to stay in a situation that isn't right and won't improve is pointless. Be brave enough to acknowledge that and move on. Reclaim your empowerment by asking yourself what you really want and what you really deserve in life. Faith in yourself and in the universe is empowering.

Have unwavering faith that there is a greater plan and it's for the better.

Be kind to yourself when you're going through situations in your romantic life of frustrations, doubt and uncertainty. You are human, after all. Various situations affect us emotionally. It is natural and normal. It's how you come out at the other end that is important.

Positive affirmations are beneficial. Use them often every day, and use them with feeling. Make sure you mean it. Don't just state something because it may make a difference. You need to actually *feel* it and *believe* it. Empower yourself by making this practice a daily habit. Even when your days are tough and you feel really down. Words go out into the universe so make sure what you say is positive and your focus is positive. The more you say something, the more you believe and feel it. Words are a magnet. Be aware of what you're thinking and saying.

Surround yourself with anything and everything positive. When you are with a funny person, you feel their energy, you laugh. Good vibes are contagious. It's all about energy. Positive energy radiates. You know because you feel it. You get a good sense and a good feeling when you are with like-minded and down-to-earth people with a positive attitude. Let that energy elate you; let it help you create your own momentum. This is why positive people are important.

The opposite also happens when you are around negative people. You pick up on their vibes and it doesn't make you feel good. So it is important when you are dealing with heartbreak, loss or grief to make sure you allow yourself to be with positive people. Their energy will be infectious and naturally help to lift you. You may want to see them again and again. Be mindful of how things make you feel and be in tune with your emotions. This is a good way to stay empowered, especially during hard times.

Remember, too, that even though you are feeling all sorts of emotions during a difficult time, it's important to concentrate on yourself and your inner journey. The more love and nurturing you give to yourself, the stronger you become. The more your shift perspective, you more you process the fact that what is happening to you isn't as harsh as you may have thought at first. While challenging, it's allowing you to gain strength and evolve to another level of being. You become more accepting as you see the greater picture. The most significant relationship you will ever have is with yourself. It is important to put that first and to nurture it.

Rejecting and not loving yourself is far more destructive than a partner rejecting or not loving you. Never abandon yourself. Be your own number one fan. When something ends and it's painful, remember that it marks the beginning of a new you, another form of you, another part of you. When you go through something that challenges you, force yourself to get up and face the day, the unknown, the what-ifs. You are already growing just by facing that head on. So each night when you retire to bed, you can say you faced the day, that you did it. Tomorrow is another day. You're capable of dealing with each experience as it comes along, whatever it may be.

When you continue this mindset day by day and face your fears and emotions, taking your journey one step at a time, you learn to adapt and change without major struggles. You are no longer the person you were before, because not only have your circumstances changed but so have you. You may see that you feel differently, have a changed outlook on life; you may feel lighter and have more energy. Doors you never thought would open start to open. Empower yourself to close the door on the event that got you in this position and look to the future. Your past obviously happened for a reason. Usually we only understand the reason in retrospect, so simply trust the process.

When you learn to love yourself and gain perspective and clarity with yourself, the relationship you have with others may also change. Your relationship with yourself sets in motion the rapport you have with others.

Be proactive in your healing. Don't be passive and just rely on time. Use your time wisely. There is nothing wrong with trial and error. You may not always get it right the first time. Stepping up and giving something a go is courageous. Always be proud. Be in the flow and let things unfold. As humans, and as women especially, we come with a set of complex emotions.

We are not necessarily going to feel empowered twenty-four hours of every day. There are times where we are overwhelmed and tired, and it feels like the world is against us and nothing is going our way. It is in these times that being present and being open are important. You can regain your positive attitude, strength and belief just by reprogramming your perspective and being yourself.

Whenever you feel shot down over a guy-gone-wrong situation, it's important to remind yourself of what you want in life. Ask yourself: *What am I gaining by feeling this way? Why am I allowing the situation with this guy to disempower me? What can I take from the experience to re-empower myself?*

The answers to these questions will lift you up out of your funk. Only you know how you feel and why. Only you can make the choices that you feel are right for you. Whether you're feeling rejected by someone, or, alternatively, feeling bad for cutting someone loose, you must always remember that there was a reason why. If something didn't feel right, it obviously wasn't right. Honour yourself but listening to your intuition. That will always win in the end. Honouring yourself even when it hurts is the most valuable thing you can do for yourself.

Unfortunately we tend to remember the negative moments more keenly than the positive ones because we are wired that way. Remembering where the lions live is a survival mechanism that is genetically built into us. Similarly, it's all too easy to get stuck reviewing and reviewing past heartbreaks. Sometimes reliving that hurt can keep us from being totally open and vulnerable again. To allow someone 'in'.

Habits are habits because we get something we need out of them – even when they hurt us. Maybe it is our need to feel cared for that makes us feel constantly sick. Or our need to feel empathy that leads us to attract the wrong people, suffer from it and then appeal to our friends for empathy. If you want to break a habit, find out what you are getting out of your negative behaviour and seek other, healthier ways to achieve that goal. Learning is a gift, even when pain is our teacher.

Never let your past experiences harm your future. Your past can't be altered and your future doesn't deserve that punishment.

*"Gratitude For
All You Have
Comes Back in Droves."*

Chapter 9
Smashing through the Pain Threshold

Someone once said, "I never make the same mistake twice. I do it five or six times, just to be sure." And isn't that so true in love? One of the most devastating blows that you can go through is the hurt and grief when love is lost. Or when love betrays you. It is a total punch in the guts. Your heart and soul are shattered. You are lost and have to find your way back. This person who brought profound meaning to your life is no longer there and what you thought you knew is gone. It's funny how when things are good, we thank our lucky stars and smile because life has dealt us the cards we want. But when the hardship and hurt comes, suddenly we blame God or the Goddess or the Universe – we are angry at the forces that be.

What did I do to deserve this?! How can he not be the one?! Why did this happen to me?! Yet all these questions and exclamations remain unanswered. Maybe things didn't happen *to* you but *for* you. Life has its ups and its downs. It tests us in many ways. That's just how it is. Things are meant to change. We are meant to grow. How would life be if it stayed the same? It is how you handle yourself and your emotions that are most important in personal development. In particular, what do you do with your thoughts? How do you stay empowered when the world has just crumbled around you? Where do you start when life challenges you? What do you say? How do you feel? When the going gets tough, the tough need to get going. When you think differently, you can slowly start to feel differently too.

Different strategies work for different people. We are not all the same. We have different levels of emotions, ways of thinking and personalities. A first step to the road of re-empowerment is to journal your feelings. Write a diary of everything you're thinking and feeling. In your private time, tune into your deep-rooted emotions and thoughts about what is going on for you. Pour it all out to detox the wounds and release the pain. Better out than in. The more you do this, the more relief you will start to feel as it's no longer bottled inside of you, poisoning you. Express how you feel with pen and paper. Be truthful, even if it hurts. You only cheat yourself if you don't let it all out and say it like it really is. It is important to acknowledge your thoughts and feelings. The good ones and the bad ones. You are honouring a part of you by telling the truth.

Writing may also allow you to gain some perspective. It may give you clarity each time you write and vent. It is amazing how this process can assist in your healing without you even realising it. As this becomes a habit, you may start to slowly become more empowered as you start to get on top of how you feel and deal with what the situation has brought. As we are all different and each situation is different, allow yourself the time and respect to heal. Being kind to yourself is a true mark of empowerment as you are saying yourself: *Whatever I am feeling, whatever I am going through, I respect, love and understand myself and allow myself to go through the process as best I can, one day at a time.*

For some, it may feel like it takes seconds to fall in love but – after a break-up – years to get over it. Always remember: It takes as long as it takes. End of story. Days, weeks, months – there's no right or wrong. But the bottom line is, rushing through the process when you need time isn't going to solve anything or make you feel better, as there is a strong chance that if you don't go through the process of healing properly, it will bite you in the tail down the track or in your next relationship. Acknowledge and feel what you are feeling, knowing that it is okay. This step is empowering.

Say positive things to yourself. Just by changing what you say to yourself can make you feel better, slowly but surely. Turn negative self-talk into positive self-talk:

Negative: *I can't believe this! I hate what has happened to me.*

Positive: *This is difficult, yes, but I will learn and come to understand that it has happened for a divine reason. This too shall pass.*

Negative: *I feel rejected, unloved and ugly.*

Positive: *I know how to rock on with a fabulous pair of stilettos and a hot outfit to match. I look amazing and he looks redundant.*

If we just incorporate the positive as soon as the negative thoughts come into our minds, it will start to become a habit. The important thing is to catch the thought before it begins to engulf your mind and emotions. It is so easy to spiral into negative patterns. Especially when your heart is broken and you are so down. But if you keep making positive changes, you begin to feel good about who you are and what you want to do with this life-changing time in your life. This could be a signal that you need to reassess what you want, what you have been meaning to do and how you see life. Let go of what is no longer serving you, let go of the old. Memories become just that – memories – as you move forward into a new journey.

Affirmations go a long way. It's interesting how positive thoughts and feelings often begin to stick. You are not going to feel empowered twenty-four hours of every single day. There are going to be many times where life situations get the better of you. Re-focusing and being present in the moment is important. The only thing that will ground you and allow you to be calm enough to focus is, in fact, the present moment. In the life of a single, it is an important exercise to ask yourself often: *What do I want? What am I gaining from this? How do I feel? Do I want to continue this relationship? Is it bringing out the best in me or not?*

Empowering questions give you clarity and lead to answers. Whether the relationship you are in is long or brief, it's not about anyone else – just you and your partner. Even if you may feel bad for cutting someone loose, if it doesn't feel right, it's not. And that's okay. You have to honour yourself and your intuition by listening to your inner voice and not the voice of others. That is the most valuable thing you can do. Honour thyself. Now that is empowering.

When you're in the dating circus and it's not going as you'd hoped, or uncomfortable patterns are starting to emerge, there is always a way to explain and let your partner know that it isn't working for you. If, for example, his behaviour or bad habits don't sit well with you, or if your requirements or expectations aren't being met, don't waste your time. If he is aware of your discontent yet isn't making changes or isn't trying to understand your point of view, this is your wake-up call. Walk away and delete his phone number. Harsh, perhaps, but ultimately you are saving yourself time, energy, tears and needless frustration, as he will never be what you want him to be.

If a man is not respectful of your time, your feelings and you as a woman, put those stilettos on and start walking.

Here's an example. Kelly met a distinguished man at the top end of his profession. He was smart and sexy and the chemistry was amazing between them. The downfall was that over the phone he'd tell her about his plans, dreams and what they would do on the weekend – then she wouldn't hear from him! He would say, "Let's go for a drink on Saturday; it's going to be a great day. And maybe Sunday we can catch a movie. I have the weekend free." But then he wouldn't follow through. He would tell her how he felt about her and what he wanted. Yet after that conversation, the weekend call and plans never came to fruition. A week later he'd text to say, "Hey, honey, missing you."

What the – ?

Clearly this was a guy who was very good at talking the talk but awful at walking the walk. Red flags started to fly and Kelly had had enough. He was not a good prospect; he was someone who loved the idea of romance but just couldn't be bothered following through with it. He liked to make it all sound good, but in the end had very little to show for it. Genius work from an ego touched by narcissism. Suffice it to say, Kelly deleted his number and moved on to someone else – a man who not only called and picked up the phone but would also pick her up, take her out and follow through on their plans.

"For every minute you remain angry, you give up sixty seconds of peace of mind."

– RALPH WALDO EMERSON

"Making Someone Responsible for Your Happiness Will Never Give You the Happiness You Seek."

TEYMARA ANTONIO WRIGHT

Chapter 10
Unrequited Love

According to Wikipedia, "Unrequited love or one-sided love is love that is not openly reciprocated or understood as such by the beloved. The beloved may not be aware of the admirer's deep and strong romantic affection, or may consciously reject it."

Ah, yes, the angst of wanting and loving someone who doesn't love you back. Bad for the heart. Great for the waistline. If you have ever wanted to get into a pair of skinny jeans, just fall in love. Much easier than going to the gym.

Or is it?

Unrequited love is a hard situation. One's mind begins to run at a hundred miles an hour. Just thinking about him gives you jittery feelings due to the mind concocting all these moments in time that you see him, are with him and are happy. Yet again it's that *Crazy. Stupid. Love.* That's what it is because you actually feel like you are going crazy. It's a hormonal imbalance. It has to be. How else do you explain it? You think obsessively about what the object of your affection is doing: *Is he thinking of me?*

Does he feel the same? Maybe if we run into each other, he'll start to see how great I am and fall for me!

The level of conversation you have in your mind doubles as you try to reason through your infatuation. You dream of what you would do together . . . The things you would say . . . Holding hands . . . The house you'll buy together . . . The exotic holidays . . . The declarations of love . . .

Time to wake up.

Unrequited love makes you go weak at the knees. There is an internal fatal attraction going on. It's funny how when you develop feelings for someone, your outlook and thinking changes. You see them differently as it corresponds to how you feel. You look forward to bumping into them. You want to call them for no real reason but just to hear their voice. The wishing, the daydreaming, the hoping.

But the thing is, this 'magical moment' is happening to *you* only – not him.

This can be a difficult pill to swallow. Many have gone through this roller coaster ride. For some it has lasted a short while and for some a long while. Some people harbour a secret love for years and years and never say anything or do anything. It's a secret love that will live in their hearts because it's safe, they're safe and it won't ruin or destroy anything or anyone. A woman's heart can swim in a river of secrets. You don't want to feel that way, but sometimes you can't help it. It is what it is. The heart wants what it wants.

There comes a time, however, when you realise that you can't live like that anymore. The unrequited feelings and mounting stress and anxiety get you nowhere. You've become lost in an unhealthy dream that will never transpire. The light bulb moment eventually does come when you realise that you are only hurting yourself and this is not something that is good for you. You are deserving of better. You're worthy of the love you desire. But as you aren't getting it from that person, you should turn inward and give it to yourself.

Stop seeing this unattainable man as the be-all and end-all. If he wanted you, nothing would stop him. He would be pursuing you. Is he calling? Is he making plans with you? If he sees you just as a friend, do yourself a favour and *accept* that. Recognising that reality allows yourself to make room for the man who *is* right for you, who wants to be with you and who is on his way.

After all, why would you want to be with someone who doesn't want you?

A good relationship should be effortless in the beginning and flow without angst and chase. Coming to terms with something that isn't going to happen can be hard, but in doing so, you empower yourself to move forward. It is important to always feel good about yourself. So why put yourself in a situation that is causing you heartache and anxiety?

Ask yourself, is he worth it? What exactly do you love about him? What are the good and not-so-good qualities you see in him? When in the grips of unrequited love, you put the object of your obsession on a pedestal. You see him as a demigod who can do no wrong. The object of your affection is perfect. Nothing bothers you about him. He is the best thing since sliced bread.

Unrequited love blinds you because that man's not real – he's a projection of what you want him to be. It's all part of an infatuation, a hormonal tsunami inside of you. That is why it is so important to stay focused on who you are and what you really want and deserve. It is very easy to get caught up in feelings. They can just creep up on you and you aren't aware that things are changing in you. Then it hits you like a ton of bricks. The agony and the ecstasy.

The best thing to do is let go. It's hard but incredibly freeing. It is always painful when the object of your affection doesn't feel the same way about you as you do about them. Your self-esteem and confidence get shot down. The downward spiral of rejection is a difficult one. You imagine if one person rejects you, then others will too. But that couldn't be further from the case. He's *one* man, not every man. That is an important distinction to remember. One guy doesn't mean all guys.

After you have been shot down, the only way up is to regain your state of mind, attitude and feeling. That's when you become empowered within. Unrequited love is, in fact, a sign that you are open and ready for love. You are open to not only giving love but also receiving it. You deserve to receive it too. If love isn't being reciprocated, then take it not as rejection but as a learning curve on your journey. It is veering you onto another path with another person who will actually be right for you. Think of it this way: If this object of your affection was meant to be for you, then wouldn't he be with you? Hold yourself in high regard and give yourself credit. Always be open to allowing someone into your life. If this is all you can see – this dead-end – then how are you going to notice when The One comes along?

The mistake that a lot of us make after the crash of unrequited love is to shut ourselves off from others because we can't bear to go through it all again. But the longer you keep yourself in this state, the longer you block the flow of love coming into your life.

Accepting that he doesn't feel the same is hard. Especially when you can so vividly picture your happy future with this person. Give that love back to yourself. Remember, if you don't love who you are, how is anyone else going to love you? Go inward and rediscover what is great about you. Put yourself first. It cannot be helped if your love isn't returned. It's part of life. It is hard not to take it personally. Of course, you do. It's the dangerous self-talk of *What is wrong with me? . . . I am not worthy of love! . . . Why doesn't he love me?* that you want to avoid at all costs! It's essential to regain your self-love by understanding that it is not you. It's just life. This *No* is someone else's *Yes*.

For every door that closes, there is another not far away that will open. It's only when you realise this that you understand that what has occurred was the right thing for you. Think of all the great people in your life who love you, and think about why they love you. Think of the things you love about your life already. Empower yourself to look at the bigger picture rather than self-sabotaging yourself with negative self-talk. It is more hurtful when you continue to focus on the door that is shut rather than looking forward to newer and better things. It does take time to move on but doing so is better for you. Life does things for a reason. Loving yourself regardless of what happens to you is the most rewarding and fundamental thing you can do for yourself. This will get you through the good times and the tough times in your life.

Love isn't easy. It's how you process those situations that happen to you that matters. Unrequited love is like fire to the heart. Mourning something that will never come to pass is something that has to be accepted. Your feelings are up and then down. It's okay.

When you are in the grips of letting go, you slowly begin to understand that when you flow with the universe in all its glory, you appreciate that people are put in your path for a reason, whether it's for a short stint or a lifetime. Even if it didn't work out and you were left broken-hearted, send him 'light and love' anyway – silent good wishes. He may have indirectly taught you patience, tenacity and awakening, something you may not have had before. Make space in your mind and heart for the infinite possibilities life can offer. In time you will see with more clarity that the bigger picture is far better than the limited view you had. Entrusting the universe is empowerment in itself as you aren't attached to the outcome. All will be as it should be. This was just part of your ride.

"I love you. You love her. Fuck this shit."

– ANON.

"Your Stilettos Can Not Only Do the Walking, But Also the Talking."

Chapter 11
Thirty-Something Questions

It is inevitable that when you enter your thirties, many new thoughts begin to fester. There is something about the big three-oh that brings up a lot in a girl.

What am I doing with my life? What do I want? Why don't I have it yet?!

There is nothing wrong with asking and thinking these questions once you hit your thirties. We all have personal goals and life ambitions. It is a normal process. For some, it's about cultural expectations. For others, it's because they thought that by a certain age they would have certain things and be living a certain life. For some, these thoughts are difficult to put aside. Most girls have desires they want or goals they hoped to achieve by thirty. Some question their current state, plagued by fears about the future. It may be about their career, finances, relationships or having children. Women feel pressure to follow the 'rules' society has mapped out for how a woman's life should unfold. When we do reach a certain age, it somehow triggers an 'OMG moment', like a quarter-life crisis.

Will I ever find a partner? Will I have children? I'm not getting any younger. Will it be too late? What if Mr Right doesn't come – then what? How long will I be waiting for The One? Will I ever have a house? A family? A better position at work?

The end of your twenties and entry into the thirties can be an overwhelming time. So many women battle with these heavy questions. Thinking through what you want out of life is key during this period of transition. But be careful. A preoccupation with the thought of 'lack' can start to dominate your focus. It can take over your emotional, mental and physical self. This state of being can also be a hindrance to possible dates. The more desperate or eager you are to get your thirties' goals on track, the more you may bring up life-goals and marriage and babies during a date, which, of course, will most likely make your date want to run for the hills. When you are relaxed and allow things to flow, you will be amazed how things just come to you when they are meant to. Often without warning. When you are so fixed on the ticking of that biological clock, you may find that you aren't attracting anything as you are fighting against the process of time, not going along with it.

You may be dating but not attracting in the right things because you are in the mindset of lack, desperation and anxiety. Anxiety because you think it's going to be too late to have those things you haven't yet attained. But who sets the age for each milestone – such as a serious relationship, marriage, babies, a mortgage and career? Is it magazines? Generations before us? Storytellers? Movies? If it's not you, then why are you listening to those voices?

It is important to know what you want and acknowledge it. If your goals aren't being met, recognise that feeling. But give yourself a time limit. It is difficult, but daydreaming strips you away from the present moment and what you have now. Focusing on the things you lack is not going to bring them into your life.

Remember, thoughts attract! If you focus on lack, that's what you'll invite.

If you are single and you desire love, marriage and children, recognise that it's important to let go of any controlling mindsets that are driven by an overwhelming sense of lack. Let go of what you can't control. You can't control everything. Nor what the universe has planned for you in its divine time. You don't know what's around the corner. So why the panic?

For too many, the focus is on *age* and the expectations that are placed on themselves instead of *living* in the present and enjoying each stage. *Why hasn't it happened? When will I find The One? What if I don't? What happens when I can't have kids or can't fall pregnant? I can't believe this relationship didn't work. Now I have to start all over again. Now what?*

Don't panic – when you panic, you make decisions that are bad for you and won't help you achieve your long-term goals. Panic can push you into making hasty decisions or can lead you to settle for what is available rather than what is best for you. Don't make fear the ruler and the reason.

Many of us know women who settled for Mr Right Now instead of waiting for Mr Right, and for all the wrong reasons. They may wake up one day with the ring on their finger, the white-picket fence and the babies, but then wonder, *Is that all there is?*

Or worse – be unhappy.

They settled to have that life they thought they wanted, without waiting for the right guy. But now they are finding that life with the wrong person is far more painful than life on their own. Making decisions out of fear or panic is never a good idea. It may very well lead to the wrong choices. Just because you don't have something yet it doesn't mean you aren't going to get it. Letting go allows you to embrace what life has to offer in many other ways.

Let go and let love – surrender to your higher self.

Getting into the mindset of gratitude, love and openness is important. When you embrace the stage of life that you are in and you let go of the angst, it is amazing what can happen. Suddenly the pressure is off and optimism and opportunity flood in. You are open to what the universe has to offer. Even if life isn't what you thought it was going to look like, you begin to accept life as it is and feel more in harmony with yourself and the world around you.

The thirties can be the decade of hardship, triumphs and challenges for many women as they become the women they want to be. Some marry and have children. Some are single. Some relationships end. Some women raise children on their own. Many are establishing careers while living and experiencing various dating dilemmas. It can be a roller coaster and a juggling act.

While many watch their friends marry and have children at this stage of life, those who haven't yet settled down can see this decade as a period of discovery, growth and experience. Seeing it from this perspective can be a big plus. Not being weighed down by commitment, responsibilities and nappies comes with its own benefits. You can embrace your freedom and use it to create and experience so much more that life has to offer. You are free to experience other paths in life, govern your own time and make your own decisions.

The thirties can be a time to grow into your own and learn to love yourself. Flaws and all. You learn what is important and what to let go of. Challenges aren't fun. They test you, push you and hurt you. But they also shape you, teach you, take you to new places and let you experience new things.

Life is about evolving.

At twenty-five, you are not the woman you are at thirty-five. Nor what you will be at forty-five. Perspective changes as you grow. Everyone goes through different experiences at different stages. We all have times of flourishing and times of difficulty. Sometimes we feel unfulfilled and question our purpose and journey. Sometimes we seek answers to what we want and what we desire. Sometimes we search for love, particularly if the past has given us heartbreak and sorrow. It is a pivotal decade of choices, responsibilities, questions, searching and finding yourself. Life tests you. Love will test you. Your thirties lay the foundations of your future. A different level of maturity starts to come in, with ideas and dreams and a different level of understanding.

Do not fear change. Don't fall into the 'that hasn't happened for me yet' way of thinking. Set yourself free emotionally and mentally from the things you think you should have by your thirties because there's no rulebook or timeline. Be grateful for all the things you do have – and never ever focus on what hasn't arrived yet. Empower yourself and allow space for more abundance in your life. You can have the things you want. It all starts with you. Surrender and have faith that what is meant for you will show up. Let the focus on your age be a thing of the past. It's just a number. It has no bearing on your happiness, spirit, soul and essence.

Empower yourself by embracing what life is giving you. The good, the bad and all in between. Love yourself enough to let go and not put unnecessary pressure on yourself. You are not a failure if you haven't reached a certain goal at a certain time. Everyone is worthy of a good life and a life they want and, of course, of love. Who said there was a cut-off age?

As the gorgeous actress and photojournalist Gina Lollobrigida once said, "A woman at twenty is like ice, at thirty she's warm and at forty she is hot."

"People Come and Go.
It's the Relationship
with Yourself that
Will Stay Forever."

Chapter 12
Mind the Gap –
from Heartbreak to Happiness

Letting go of something that was once cherished and significant is one of the most challenging things one can do. For many who believe in 'forever', it's a hard thing to fathom when it's over. From the moment it happens, you feel lost and don't know where to start to begin again. The gap of time between devastation to healing to dating again varies from person to person and situation to situation.

So what happens in the gap between heartbreak to happiness?

A journey of self-discovery. It's a process of taking the time to figure out who you are, where you are and what you want to do next – what you want to be now that life is taking you in another direction. It is a blank page from which to create and build a new life.

Starting again sounds overwhelming. It's taking the initial step and dealing with all the emotions that come with it. There is no manual to mending a broken heart. It takes time, strength and courage to love again and keep moving forward. How do you even fathom dating again when your heart has been shattered? How do you find your spark and start again?

They say the journey of a thousand steps starts with the first one. It's allowing yourself the space, time and the opportunity to rediscover who you are. It's giving yourself permission to grieve and to let go of all the heavy baggage of anger, resentment and bitterness. To move on properly, these things must dissolve. Carrying around negative feelings isn't going to help you or make you feel good. It is excess baggage. Filter through your emotions and take the time necessary to process all that is required for you to move on mentally and emotionally. You don't want old feelings tainting your fresh blank canvas.

So before you are ready to paint your new picture for your future, allow the process and filtering of emotions to come to the surface so you can deal with them one by one. This is most probably the hardest part and may take some time. But your heart will eventually heal. Then you can go on and have a heart that is free, joyful and open to new doors and opportunities that come your way. You may even look back and be thankful that it turned out the way it did. You may even be thankful for the lessons and how the experience changed you. Nothing is ever an accident. Even the things we don't like or want to experience. But life is both positive and negative. The two go hand in hand. You can't experience happiness without sadness. You have more of an appreciation for happiness in times of sadness. If you really tried, even in the most difficult times, you can still find something to be thankful for. When you stop asking *Why?* you can begin to ask *What next?*

Trying to make sense of an ending is hard and so is the prospect of a new chapter in your life. But usually once you start with a new chapter, you tend to continue on with it. You keep going. You can't stop a chapter halfway.

What about betrayal? How do you trust again when what you thought was real was a lie? The motions of anger, sadness, resentment and bitterness all manifest as you try and process the *how* and *why* when life pulls the rug out from under you. You may feel these emotions strongly and for some time. That is natural and understandable. But bottling them inside is not healthy for your mental, emotional and physical state of being. Feel these emotions and understand them. Acknowledge that they are there. Don't push them away or bury them.

There are many avenues one can take to assist in dealing with this kind of heartbreak. Having positive and supportive friends and family is a blessing as it allows you to talk about it. For some, yoga and meditation can do wonders. For others, speaking to a counsellor, spiritual healer or life coach may be what they need to gain perspective. There are many ways to reach out and give yourself the permission to process and heal. Love yourself and help yourself. Working through negative emotions is important.

While travelling from that place of grieving into a place of healing, you may discover things about yourself that you weren't aware of, such as your strengths and weaknesses; how you view things; your perceptions of life, love and other people. You may discover things about people that you didn't know before, such as who your real friends are or whom can be relied upon. Has the behaviour of some people changed towards you because of this?

Inevitably, you see life differently than before because life has changed. You are in the process of evolving and learning about yourself, your likes and dislikes. What you will tolerate and what you won't. You learn about the things that make you happy and the things that make you sad. You reflect on what you would do differently the next time around. If you could change something, what would it be? You might handle yourself differently than before. You may make new friends and let go of old friends or people you thought were your friends but really weren't true. You let go of toxic people and things that no longer serve you as you become stronger and confident again.

Not every day will be a good day while you are going through the process of healing and building yourself up again. Take each day as it comes. Allow yourself to have a crappy day when it comes. Sometimes you need to allow yourself a moment of weakness and vulnerability in order to grow stronger. On those days, try getting centred and still.

Yoga and meditation have been shown to have huge benefits in assisting overall well-being. Treat yourself on those days. Do something that makes you feel great. It could be something simple like sitting on your own and having a latte in a café near the beach. It could be watching a funny movie or taking a swim.

Looking out for yourself is primary. Learning to be happy in your own company is pivotal in order to be happy with someone else. Learn to be happy with alone time. This may sound daunting to some, especially if you have been used to being with someone and now they aren't there anymore. It's a bit like Brussels sprouts. No one really likes them or the even thought of them. But made right with the right seasoning, they can taste damn fine. See your alone time as that. Done correctly, you can have a blast. You get used to it, just like the taste of

Brussels sprouts. Then you become comfortable with it and learn to enjoy it (just like sprouts became a staple side when Mum makes her lamb roast on Sundays!).

This may sound like a strange concept to grasp, but date yourself. Why don't you date you? Only you know what you like and how you feel. Get to know you again before you get to know someone else. That way when you do get to know someone else, you're giving them the best version of you – the you that you love and know. How wonderful does it feel to give to you? Love thyself and know thyself. What better way to get through this challenging time? Use the time from heart-break to happiness to reconnect with yourself. Remind yourself that you are a great person and worthy of great things. Even to love again. When you date yourself, the world is your oyster! You can do whatever you like, whenever you like. Nothing is holding you back. Do the things you love. Maybe try things you have always wanted to try but haven't been able to do. The only thing that would hold you back is your own mindset.

When you go from a 'we' to an 'I' and it is still uncomfort-able, write down all the things that are great about doing things for yourself and write all the things you like to do. Not every-thing has to be done as a duo. Try it solo. The first few times may be hard but it will become second nature after a while. Accepting and adapting to a new way of life is the key to slowly moving forward. Make it a habit to do something thoughtful and nice for yourself a few times a week. It could be running a bath and listening to music. It could be a nice flower arrange-ment on your table. It could be hosting a dinner party. Whatever floats your boat. It is your life and your time now. You may also inadvertently start to regain some self-confidence and belief in yourself that had been stripped from you before.

Some say that the stage in between heartbreak to happiness is a strange one. And it actually is. You have ups and downs. Feeling down isn't a great way to be. Sometimes all we are seeking is validation that we are beautiful, lovable and worthy. Your self-esteem is shot because the one person you loved and the life as you knew it is now gone. We've all heard the saying, "The way to get over someone is to get under someone else." Okay, that doesn't work for all of us, but it works for some.

No judgement. No shame.

Some just need that pick-me-up feeling – the validation that you are still desirable and have what it takes, which is something that heartbreak steals from you. A fling can be about no attachments, no real emotional feelings, no explanations. Just giving into inhibitions and taking a step and allowing yourself to be with another, regardless of how long you have known them or not. Having fun and letting yourself be. Allowing yourself to feel alive again in the tsunami of emotions that has engulfed you. It can be a little confirmation that you've 'still got it'.

One-night stands can be a reaction for some, not just as an expression of being free and open to opportunities, but an attempt to numb the pain. You can mistakenly think that you are moving on when really you aren't. They can be the drug that brings your emotions in check and make you feel alive, energised and happy. The first time with someone else can be a little unnerving. You might actually wonder if you can pull it off. *Can I do it? Do I still know how to do it? Will he judge the size of my bum?* We are our own worse critics as we play around with these thoughts in our head. There's nothing wrong with wanting to feel good and allowing yourself the freedom to be desired intimately by a man. It is liberating and flattering, especially if you have been with someone for so long and you want to know what else is 'out there'.

Participating in flings is a really personal choice as we are all different, feel different and react differently. It's about your core values and how you wish to process your feelings, emotions and your life at the time. You may have a few one-night stands and come to realise that they don't truly provide you with what you want, that you deserve more and want more. It is really dependent on the person and where you are at emotionally, spiritually, mentally and physically in your life. Whatever the reason, whether it's escape, validation or just fun, everyone needs to do what's right for them. The flip side is that it could make you feel worse than before. If you're doing it to numb the pain, it may prompt you to think, *Why am I doing this? What am I achieving? Am I just hurting myself?*

After being shattered in love, it's natural that something inside you would crave validation, acceptance and admiration. You are hurt, exposed and vulnerable. Like you have been stripped bare. Mandy, a single woman in her late thirties, had broken up with her partner of five years due to infidelity on his part. She was beyond broken as she never thought her life would turn out the way it did. "I was a mess," she recalls. "Emotionally I didn't know where I was and what to do. It was a roller coaster. I was angry and hurt that I was living a lie. Someone I had never lied to was lying to me.

"I felt unworthy and my self-esteem was low. It took a while, but I just met a guy and I didn't want any emotional connection or to really see him on a dating level. So I began sleeping with him. It felt wonderful. I felt empowered and proud that I could have sex without attachment and be fine with it. I didn't care. So I guess I was trying to prove something to myself. It was like a 'stuff you' to my ex for hurting me. This went on for a while, then it fizzled out. I had to get it out of my system, I guess. But in all honesty, for me, sex with feeling and attachment is better. There is more meaning. The former is just emptiness in the end."

Are you longing to feel someone next to you? Have you mourned the past and are still in the process of rediscovery? There are many layers to this and the 'why' differs for many people. It could be a reaction to anger. *Stuff this – he hurt me! I don't care anymore. Guys are bastards. I'm just going to enjoy myself. Who cares? Men do it, so why shouldn't we?* In which case, of course, your motivations for a fling are the wrong ones and will probably cause you more hurt.

One-night stands are a personal choice so there is no right or wrong answer. It is part of the process and is exercised for the reason of the individual. They are what they are and can play a part in the development, discovery and growth of a person. It all forms part of the journey and some lessons need to be repeated in order to be understood. We all stumble many times in our quest for love, but those 'mistakes' teach us and give us more insight and knowledge about how we want to be in relationships, what we want in relationships and about you responding to the cause and effect of what love can do. You never really lose the lesson. You can't change what has been done but can only move through it and rise above it. It may take a few goes, but you eventually will get there.

> *"It's been too long since I felt the mortifying regret of a one-night stand."*
>
> — ANON.

*"Don't Think
You Are Amazing –
You Are Amazing."*

Chapter 13

The Grass Is Always Greener

How is it that our perception can get so muddled? Maybe the movies have a lot to do with it – when we see a man go out of his way to get his woman, win her over then ride into the sunset. You see them happy, laughing and smiling from ear to ear. They have a beautiful home with a dog and maybe a kid or two. They seem to be living the dream and having it all. The grass is so freaking green, they need a new name for that shade of green. Why is that?! She is the doting missus and he is the loving hubby who goes to work and is always home for dinner. It seems too good to be true, doesn't it? It is happening around you, yet this fabulous fantasy life isn't happening to you. You wonder if the dream of having this wonderful life could ever happen. Okay, wake up now.

When you look at your friends or family members, neighbours or colleagues and see them all lovey-dovey, you can't help but think, How did she get so lucky? I guess this is just my lot in life. Bad relationships, time after time. I'm just unlucky in love.

It is a thought process that carries on somewhat instantly. Especially when it comes to an area of our life that probably hasn't flourished as you'd hoped. By looking at someone's 'greener lawn', you not only feel discouraged, you may even feel personally lacking, bringing out unnecessary insecurities and worries. We all know that when something is new and fresh, it is exciting and joyous. Everything is wonderful. Of course, it is how you sustain things as time goes on that counts. But when looking at other people's relationships, we often only focus on how things look from the outside. Your perception becomes blurred as you think that what is on the outside is reflected on the inside. Whereas it may not be all that well and good in reality. What goes on behind the closed doors can be a whole different picture. Empower yourself to see the bigger picture, as the superficial perspective can often be all smoke and mirrors. Empower yourself to keep an open mind. Redirect that longing to have what so many others seem to have and instead focus on all you do have. Practising gratefulness will help you keep positive momentum in your life and to create the life you want. No one is perfect and there is no perfect relationship, so it's worthwhile to consider the complete picture.

The stolen kiss or shared joke between a couple at a barbecue is part of a much bigger picture, a complicated tapestry of who they are as a duo. Rome wasn't built in a day and things like relationships take time to evolve. We all have our own ways of being. Looking at friends or other people who seem to 'have it all' adds no positive energy to you. It's just envy and wishful thinking.

Empower yourself by looking within and dreaming about what you want in life. Figure out how you can master your passions. What do you like? What do you want in a partner?

How do you see your relationships? How do you want to feel? Don't wish yourself away by looking at other couples and measuring them with the 'got it all' meter. Every couple is different. What works for them may not work for you. Create your own greener pastures by mapping out what you want and what you don't want in your life. Envision what your greener grass looks like. You may have a great relationship. What would that look like for you? How do you feel about your life and your beliefs? What are your core values that you may need to assess or tap into?

The way to water your own garden is to focus on your own life, not anyone else's. The more you do things to improve, change or adjust your life, the greener it will become and you'll start attracting what you want. This is a way of giving back to yourself when you feel less than or when you get into that state of looking at someone else's seemingly perfect life. When you are not experiencing the things you want at that present time, it is easy to get caught up in the 'what-ifs' and the 'why not me' kind of thinking. Remember that we all have different journeys in life and we all have a purpose and destiny. But timing is everything. Things fall into place as they are meant to. The trick is for you to start creating and doing the things you want to in life – to become not only the star of your life but also the producer and director.

Instead of looking at the greener grass and feeling envy that it hasn't happened to you, look at those relationships as examples of where you want to be and what you would like to have. See it as a blueprint of what you'd like to create and have in your life. Instead of measuring yourself against others, therefore creating negative energy centred around 'lack', use them as a guide to forming the kind of relationship or situation that you want to attract. Change the way you look at it. Water your own grass and plant your own seeds rather than looking at what others 'seem' to have. You would be amazed at what can happen.

Thinking the grass is greener takes the shine from your own life and the focus away from the things you should be grateful for. Embrace your own life. Your dreams, accomplishments, desires and intentions. Who said you can't get a better job, a nice house, and a great relationship? Constantly looking at others and their accomplishments will only make you feel bad. So stop looking in their backyard. Do the opposite.

Nurture your own garden.

Be clear on what you want and how you feel and be passionate about what you do. This is the pathway to not only finding inner harmony but also getting the greener grass that you have wanted.

Empower yourself to not look at others' lives and wish yours away. We are all on a different playing field. Empower yourself to focus in on you and the things that bring you joy and what you want to achieve. You would be surprised to see what happens when you start to get a life, so to speak, and change your state of thinking. Empower yourself to appreciate your life and the things in it. Being into yourself on a mental and spiritual level is one of the most important things you can do for you. You begin to live more in the present moment.

Have faith as you go, for all is possible. You attract what you are meant to attract for the right reason and lesson.

Who knows – maybe others look at the freedom in your life and see *your* grass as greener. We all want what we don't have. Instead of feeling that loss of the unattainable, begin to create the attainable. Even in the little things. Meeting people through networking, sports activities, hobbies and interests or volunteering. Connecting is the way to start the ball rolling. Just relax. Let go of the 'I don't have' and start creating the 'I have'.

> *"A competent and self-confident person is incapable of jealousy in anything. Jealousy is invariably a symptom of neurotic insecurity."*
>
> – ROBERT A. HEINLEIN

> *"Sometimes our thoughts are backed by so much insecurity, that they create lies we believe."*
>
> – ANON

*"You Can be
What You Want.
Just Believe It."*

Chapter 14
Dress for Success

When one has been faced with the loss and devastation of a break up yet has slowly but surely been rebuilding the pieces of their emotional, spiritual, mental and physical life, the next step may feel either daunting or exciting: dating!

Being single means you are free to do and be absolutely anything you want. If you feel like going out, you can. If you don't want to, you don't. It's really simple and you have control over everything you do. Everyone takes their own time and space to heal. There comes a time where you make decisions about where you want to be in life and what direction you want to take it in.

When you are ready to date again, you allow yourself the chance to be open to love again. There may be nerves and hesitations, but it gets easier after a few initial first dates and you become more comfortable with being out there, vulnerable and open. In your past relationship, you may have felt as though you jumped straight in, so as you re-enter the dating world, you may want to take it slow, like dipping your toe in the ocean. For those who haven't dated in some time due to being in a long-term relationship, they may initially feel like a fish out of water, as times have changed dramatically. The digital age has shifted our behaviours and approach to dating.

Some things never change, however. We all still aspire to make a good impression, look good and present ourselves well when meeting someone new. It can be exciting to get ready for a date. Particularly if it is someone you have already connected with and now you are actually meeting one-on-one. What do you wear? You want to look nice. So where do you start? There are a lot of questions and what-ifs that go on inside your head. Everyone wants to make a good impression (even men!).

The most important part of this is how you see yourself and how comfortable you are in your own skin. Being happy with who you are is an important factor. If you are happy with yourself, it will show and certainly play a role in how others see you too. However, you don't just want to impress with your outer beauty – your inner self is what ultimately matters, so allow the real you to shine. There's no reason why you can't have both inner and outer attractiveness, but you don't want to present yourself as someone you're not, or project yourself falsely in any way. Men want real women. So find your confidence by looking within.

When you have risen from the ashes and are in a great mental and emotional space, you feel good and you want to show that to the world. The most important key is to use your *je ne sais quoi* – your certain something – which comes more from self-confidence than anything else. If you are happy and confident in yourself as a woman, whatever you wear will be further enhanced, no matter where you are going.

So the next question is: What do you wear on a first date? It all depends, of course, on where you are going. Is it a dinner? A cocktail at a rooftop bar? A movie and a coffee? Let's say, for instance, it's a dinner date at a bistro. Perhaps a little black dress will do the trick, adding a splash of colour with some strappy stilettos and a twinkle to the décolletage with a necklace. Alternatively – for a more sophisticated look – a pencil skirt to the knee with a blouse with a plunging neckline and, again, a nice pair of heels.

You want to look stylish and a little sexy too. Men are visual creatures so give them a little but not a lot. If you want to accentuate the neckline, wear a skirt that is to the knee or pants that are either tightly fitted or tailored. If you want to accentuate the legs, then perhaps wear a top that doesn't reveal the bust so much, such as a sleeveless shirt or a pretty blouse. Sophisticated style will emphasise one part of the body at a time, not both – unless you're trying to send a different message altogether and have him staring at your assets all night, rather than your eyes. Pick an asset and accentuate it. If it's the top you want to enhance or an off-the-shoulder look, wear a more conservative skirt or pants; if it's legs you're emphasising, then choose a more concealing top.

It is not always what you wear but how you wear it and how you work it on your date. This will capture his attention. You want to visually capture his curiosity and his eye, and at the same time you want to engage in communication and connection. For instance, if you are in a casual environment for your date, a laid-back approach to your attire may be better. Too dressed up may send the wrong message or you may appear to be trying too hard to impress. Jeans are so versatile and they are a staple piece in everyone's wardrobe. Pair them with a plain top and a blazer with mid-length heels, boots or ballet flats. A chilly night? Maybe opt for a scarf or a long coat or a stylish trench coat. Layer if you would like to. An off-the-shoulder baggy jumper that shows your singlet or top underneath with a cashmere wrap is a sexy, casual look. If your jumper or top is a block colour (black, grey, blue, white), then add a wrap or scarf to splash on some colour or a pattern. This will draw attention. If it is a balmy evening and you are going waterside for a drink, consider a maxi dress with colour, some strappy sandals or wedges and a tote bag. It's casual and not overdone, particularly if it's hot you don't want to be un-comfortable. Again, it comes down to how you are feeling and learning what is good for you.

Regardless of what you wear, high heels always make an outfit. They elongate the body, add elegance and complete the look. Those few extra inches improve your posture, making you look the part. They add confidence, which is the most important element, both mentally and emotionally. The two go together. It takes courage to start again and take that step. Remember to be proud of yourself for taking that leap of faith. It may feel daunting and uncomfortable at first. Getting out of your comfort zone for any reason is awkward and feels strange and unnerving. But once you take that leap and follow your inner voice, you will start to get into the flow again, and you will learn more about yourself in the process. Especially in the dating game. You always have the power and the control. Always. Don't put pressure on yourself. There's no hurry.

First impressions count so it's most ideal to set the date in a laid-back environment where you can feel relaxed, as it's easy to pick up on someone else's energy. The ambience and connection go hand and hand. Every date and situation is different. There may be an awkward moment. You may laugh during one date and yawn through another. Things may start well, followed by a topic in which you disagree or that rubs you the wrong way. It is important to adapt and be open to the moment. Always be clear and be yourself. Not every guy you meet will take your breath away. Forget rom-coms and romance novels – they are only stories designed to ignite the imagination. Don't have too many expectations in the beginning, other than putting your best foot forward and being yourself. Early dates are just simply about enjoying the company and conversation as you get to know someone. Have a laugh and don't take things too seriously. Be flexible. If you start the date with a huge checklist in your head of things he must be and what he must have, then you are setting yourself up for disappointment. Throw out your checklist and just go with the flow. You have already taken the step of putting yourself out there, so that's kudos to you!

Once you are comfortable with how you look and feel, everything begins to fall into place. What you wear is only part of the way you feel and what you project. The way you carry yourself is most important. Work with what you have without trying too hard. Be happy and be confident in your abilities. All you can be is the best version of yourself and that's the best thing you can bring to the date. Authenticity goes a long way. Don't be afraid.

Remember what some of the best fashionistas have said . . .

"Fashion is . . . about something else that comes from within you."

— RALPH LAUREN

"Style is a way to say who you are without having to speak."

— RACHEL ZOE

Amen, sister.

"If the Shoe Fits,
Wear It . . .
And Wear It Well."

Chapter 15
The Power of Self-Pampering

After being in a relationship for some time, you may find yourself compromising more than you expected, or even giving up or losing a part of who you are. It's important to take into consideration the other person and, of course, children, if they are on the scene. All of a sudden you operate more as your title than yourself. 'Girlfriend', 'wife', 'mother' – these titles start to take precedence over *you*.

When you get into the routine and flow of life and take on these roles, the *you* that you knew somehow changes and evolves. Your identity intertwines with being an 'other half' or mum. You start taking care of others before yourself. When this becomes the norm, you tend to inadvertently forget about who you are and the things you love and even start to lose your identity. At work you are responsible for your job and its requirements. At home you are the keeper and responsible for your kids and partner.

So when do you become responsible for you? Last? Late at night when you have half an hour up your sleeve before bed and it all starts again in the morning? It becomes automatic. You switch into autopilot, whether you like it or not. It's life.

But when you are newly single or it's been a while since you've dated, you now have the opportunity to get to know yourself and be comfortable in your skin. You have time to accept yourself for the total package – flaws and all – and redis-cover what you like and what you don't like. We are constantly changing so what you liked or how you felt about something ten years ago may not reflect what you feel now. You need to explore the you that is present now – the things you love, the things you miss, the things that inspire you and things you want to try that you've never done before. Explore this facet of your life. Being with yourself and being happy with who you are is important for your growth and fulfilment as a woman. You change and you adapt. So no matter what happens in your life and what form of relationship comes your way, you will always be happy with *you*. What matters in the end is that you feel complete in yourself – you're not looking for another to complete you.

So date you.

Be with you – the new you. Do new things, listen to your inner voice, take chances. Be bold as well as beautiful. Give to yourself. You can't expect others to give to you if you don't give to yourself. You will find that once you start, you will actually begin to enjoy it. An example may be taking a long pampering bubble bath once a week. Or indulging in a glass of really nice red wine. You may start a new art class on Saturdays. Mondays could be cooking your favourite meal. Fridays for a girl's night out.

You can create the life you want, where before you may not have been able to. You have the luxury and choice of creating your life any way you want it, without answering to anyone. So treat yourself when you can. Even the little things, the simple things. Walking along the beach. Starting a new sport. Buying flowers for your lounge room. Forming new habits. Starting new activities. Challenging yourself. Clear your mind of negative patterns that don't serve you.

Reassess your priorities and remember the lessons learned from the past. Make clear-headed decisions on what you'll tolerate and what you'll accept in the future. The more you get to know you and what you want, the more you will build self-confidence, awareness and standards. You may think differently about taking on a partner that doesn't suit your standards. You may be less likely to accept excuses.

When you look after yourself, you become emotionally stronger too. Give to you what you would like to be given. Let your life take shape. Dating yourself can be the best thing you can do for you. It simply translates to self-love, which is the most important basis for starting any new relationship.

> *"We don't get enough pampering. If we were once the only child of an adoring mother, we developed a taste for it; if not, we developed a thirst for it."*
>
> — BARBARA HOLLAND

> *"Always important to stop and smell the roses."*
>
> — FERRIS BUELLER

*" Self-Love is the
First Step to
True Freedom."*

– TEYMARA ANTONIO WRIGHT

Chapter 16
When Life Gives You Lemons, Make Limoncello

When you meet that someone amazing, you are synced, you gel, your attraction is sky-high and all the pieces of the puzzle seem to fit. Then as the relationship progresses, sometimes it becomes apparent that things aren't really working as you'd hoped or aren't flowing as you thought they would. The calls get shorter and less frequent. Behaviours change and undesirable characteristics come to the surface. When this happens, most of us question if these issues are just 'teething problems' that will settle in their own in time, while simultaneously we wrestle with the fear of incompatibility. That's a tricky tightrope to walk.

You can't force something to manifest and you can't make someone be a certain way. They are who they are – just as you are. What if you have given something a number of chances but to no avail and your patience has worn thin? Are you compromising your self-respect to stay in a less-than-ideal situation? Are you able to recognise when enough is enough and it's time to call it quits?

It is never easy when feelings are involved. But when your self-worth and self-respect begin to get rattled, you know you are deserving of better. The thought of breaking free can be daunting. Starting again can be frustrating. But that option is better than the one you are probably in. So when life deals you a lemon, the best thing to do is make limoncello.

In dating terms, this means getting on with living and creating a great life for yourself. Don't take it too seriously and personally. You will live . . . and you'll love again. Observe the lesson. Recognise it for what it is or was. What did that person teach you? What did they bring to you in your life experience or personal development? There is always a form of gain in a loss. Again, there are no accidents. What can you take from that experience? Don't always take the closing of a chapter as bad. Allow this perspective to take you to the now.

So you got a lemon. We all do. Sometimes you get several in life. Even a lemon can be a valuable ingredient in the overall punch bowl that adds to your balance and life experience. When the timing is right, you eventually attract the right fruit with the right perspective. Lemons help us to gain life experience; they help us grow and build strength and character. A few bad lemons won't spoil the entire bowl. Use the experience to build your path to the future, weeding out the elements you *don't* want in a relationship, the situations you *won't* put up with. Send 'love and light' – silent good wishes – to your lemon as you make lemonade from the experience. Add the 'sugar' of the insight, growth and perspective you gained from the experience so your lemonade turns out sweet – not sour. Be mindful of all that happened so you can grow from the experience, rather than being tarnished by it. Don't let a bad experience taint your next relationship.

We've all heard the saying, 'shit happens' – meaning that life is full of unpredictable events, challenges and setbacks – and this certainly applies to the dating world. You don't know what is going to come your way next. When you are out there and you have date after date – and dud after dud – it can sometimes be easy to think, *Enough is enough already. They're all lemons!* But it's all about perspective and the choice is yours: Give up and resign yourself to the life of a tracky-dack-wearing crazy cat lady . . . or pick yourself up, slap on some lippy and soldier on!

This is not always easy, of course. Sometimes you look around and see nothing but friend after friend falling in love with their soulmate, while you flounder with attracting the right person or getting into a dating rhythm that flows nicely and can evolve. Watching this go on around you in your circle of friends and family can be disconcerting and depleting to the core. So how do you stay positive when you've dated five lemons in a row?

Start by making mental clarity a priority. It is very easy to get into a state of mind-chatter and negativity. As you find yourself slipping into that depleted emotional state, acknowledge the fact that it is a normal emotional component of your inner self, but you *do* have the power to switch off this low-grade feeling. In fact, almost immediately, if you want. It takes a swift change in perspective. There is undoubtedly a reason why life threw you a lemon; maybe even a few of them. Did you attract the same issues and the same type of person? What was that issue that the universe kept throwing in your face? Have you learned the lesson yet? Don't drown in self-pity and *why me?!* Life gives challenges to every single one of us. Be conscious of the lessons and learn from them. Make lemonade with your lemons – or even a limoncello (that deliciously potent Italian liqueur) because we all need the strong stuff from time to time to cauterise the emotional wounds!

But how do we turn lemons into limoncello?

When life throws you a challenge and it feels hard to overcome, release all your anger, frustration and sadness by giving it to the universe. Acknowledge your feelings and own them – it is important not to try to switch them off. Then open the lines of perspective and realise that these struggles are part of your journey, part of the bigger picture. Each experience is a stepping stone: People, places, situations, failures, disappointments are all designed for you and your growth and life story. Some will hurt you, some will test you and most of them will open you up to new and exciting things – even if you can't see that in the moment.

Take things as they are. Try not to overthink and overwhelm yourself. The good old cliché that "what doesn't kill you makes you stronger" is very true. In that moment of hurt and vulnerability, while you're busy trying to process your situation and your feelings, that might be the last thing you want to hear. Yet that saying can be a great catalyst for changing your perspective from negative to positive. Did you get out of bed this morning? Are you healthy? Do you have food and a job and a roof over your head? Do you have clean clothes and a shower every day?

If you answer 'yes' to all of these questions, then you are doing pretty okay. A bad date or bad relationship is a setback, not a life-threatening situation. So just take a step forward now. It's as easy as one foot in front of the other.

Using your lemon to make limoncello is simply another way of looking at your current situation and letting that take you to another place, time and circumstance. Making limoncello gives you the space and time to self-heal and be open to new opportunities and allow new things to come into your life. It isn't always easy, yet it is essential in the tapestry of life. In essence, we don't stop getting lemons throughout life – they come in different forms over our lifespans, such as situations, family issues, relationships, work and so forth. Emotional maturity is the process of becoming better at dealing with lemons when they come our way, and more equipped at handling challenging situations, including romantic letdowns.

This is a part of life. It's a given. Most of us don't always get it right. But who says what is right and what is wrong? You are in charge of your life. You run your own race. The way you make your lemonade is entirely up to you. It is difficult to know how and when. We are all different. When you are in a state of elation because you've found someone you really like and you are connecting, you think about him all the time and you fantasise about what it would be like if you were together permanently. But then, in the blink of an eye, with a bad date or breakup, your dreams are crushed and that flicker of hope is gone. It is hard to know how to start processing the disappointment. But highs and lows are part of life – and also part and parcel of the dating world. So turn that lemon into limoncello by considering the following:

- When I really think about it, did he actually have all the qualities I want in a partner? Or was I projecting my desires onto someone who was never right in the first place? Maybe I dodged a bullet.
- I was able to experience places I hadn't experienced before. If I hadn't met him, I may never have experienced those things.
- There were certain things in him that I was not able to accept. I am not going to accept anything less than what I deserve.
- I am worthy of love, happiness and someone who enriches my life. I don't deserve someone who pulls me down.
- I have a divine higher purpose in life. If it was 'meant to be', it *would* have been. There is someone better suited to me to come.
- I am okay. I am strong, capable and in control of my life.
- There are far worse things in life than a bad date or failed relationship. I am grateful for all that I have and all that I am.
- I am grateful for . . . (you fill in the blanks).

Turning lemons into limoncello makes you appreciate life more. You can't change what's been done. You can only move on from it. Sometimes we make allowances and excuses for people, trying to 'sugar-coat' their behaviour. Eventually, a particular situation arises that becomes the straw that breaks the proverbial camel's back. It's only then that you see clearly and know that enough is enough and something has to change. The truth can be tricky to see while in the middle of it all. When you remove yourself from the situation and take the emotions out of it, then you see the meaning of it all and understand when something isn't meant to be. This form of perspective is an empowering thing you can do for yourself. It means actually processing the situation and moving forward. You may even take the mickey out of it and have a laugh.

Turning lemons into limoncello is the best thing you can do for yourself and the most empowering way to deal with the woes of life and love. As you make limoncello – that is, learning to transform negative feelings into valuable life experiences to develop your emotional wisdom – it gets a little easier as time goes on. It is about making the best of what you have and who you are. Always be true to yourself and don't allow a situation to overtake you, regardless of who comes into your life and who departs.

Limoncello brewing will always be a valuable tool for other subsequent disappointments that life can bring. The faster you learn to turn lemons into limoncello, the more quickly your happiness will return.

> *"I believe when life gives you lemons you should make lemonade . . . And try and find somebody whose life has given them vodka . . . and have a party."*
> – RON WHITE

> *"Lemons are a state of mind."*
> – RAHUL GANDHI

"Real Beauty
Lies Within Soul."

Chapter 17
The Single Mother's Survival Guide

When life throws you a significant curve ball – like the end of a major relationship – and there are children involved, it can be one of the most challenging and emotional experiences of your life. But a time will come when the grief and hardship finally subside and you'll be ready to get back on the wagon. But how? How do you go through the whole dating experience again while putting your children first and trying to balance your work life, family life and single life?

People and situations differ, yet for any parents aspiring to re-enter the dating world, the burning conundrum remains: Can you really have it all? How can you even try to have it all? This question lies dormant in most of us as we try to juggle responsibilities and dream of a more balanced life. It can be a hard one to fathom, yet it is something that most of us want to attain. When life deals you this card and you find yourself single again after so long, with children and some form of emotional baggage, what happens to you? How do you go back and nourish *you*? Everyone's situation, of course, varies. It may be safe to say that the emotional journey is a raw one. However, one woman's journey could resonate with many other people on various levels.

Tracey, for example, is just one of many women who re-discovered strength again after so long when she found herself separated from a difficult marriage and now having to raise two children on her own. It wasn't just that her relationship of almost twenty years had ended, it was also the sinking feeling that no one loved her anymore. Here she was, as a mother, a daughter, a friend, a colleague – yet she felt a sense of not belonging. She was no longer a wife. She was used to being 'somebody' and belonging. She defined herself this way, as many do. It was like there was a stigma she felt now that there was no ring on her finger. People would know she wasn't married. What would they think and say? It was a hard to break out of that thought process. It was a hard thing to accept that she was no longer married. The most important thing for Tracey (and many women in her position) was to make sure that her children were looked after and felt loved. She made sure there was as little disruption to their lives as possible. For her, it was about keeping the family nucleus together. That was her priority, first and foremost.

While she was managing this, she noticed the difference between being single in her later years and having children, as opposed to in her early years. It was a totally different ballgame. She recalled as she looked back that the younger years were times of immaturity. You worry about pleasing people. Pleasing the boys when they would call you back or take you out. It was like you had to be accepted and do what he liked and wanted. So much of what you do is in order to be liked and loved. Whereas now, with maturity and experience, Tracey realised it should be about healthy relationships, building and creating good foundations for a relationship, whether it be with friends, children, colleagues, family or partners. Stable relationships are fundamental in progressing into a future.

Tracey's sentiments resonate with many. The time it takes for one to be ready to re-join the dating scene differs greatly from person to person. For Tracey, it took years for her to finally allow someone new into her life.

"It was a process that happened internally," says Tracey. "To filter what had happened and get the children to a good place took time, and I did eventually meet someone and it was a lovely experience. I thought, *Wow, this is what real love is. Finally.* It was real and exciting and it was just what I needed."

Once the family nest was stable, her life begun to flow again and she gave herself permission to open up and embrace life and love again. Her story introduces a valid point to those who have gone through the devastation of divorce and grief. You need to give yourself permission to love and be open again. It is okay to give it a go. No two situations are the same. Give yourself the chance to try again. Give yourself permission to love.

For many women, even those with similar experiences to Tracey, the wedding ring symbolised many things – a unity, love, the sanctity of marriage and the bond between two people. It is there to symbolise all that binds two people in marriage. To not have that anymore can create an empty feeling. For Tracey, in the beginning she didn't like having it off. People would see she wasn't wearing it anymore and know that her marriage was over. It was difficult to face others and have to explain it to people. She really had to change the way she saw the whole thing, to not worry about what people would say or think. Other people's opinions were irrelevant in her journey. All that mattered was her own personal healing.

At that time, dating wasn't even an option in her mind. To find someone that could take on an independent woman with two children, knowing she was a passionate, determined and loyal woman, was a big ask and a hard find, she thought. She needed to meet someone who would understand. She knew it wasn't wise to jump straight into another relationship.

It is important to give yourself time to get to know yourself again and to evaluate who you are and what you want. Give yourself space. Are you ever ready? Only you know. Process the end of something before you start something new. It can take a long time, but it's not a race and there is no time limit. You never know until you know. You have to be happy within yourself. If someone can add value to your life then, yes, but if it brings you down and you find it difficult, then you should wait a little longer before dating again. If you are juggling mother-hood, obviously children should be your highest priority.

"Be there for your kids," Tracey explains. "Build the foundation. There is never an age in childhood where they don't need you. Make them a priority, especially after a divorce. Keep that most important relationship strong and secure. Eventually they may even be the ones encouraging you to meet someone new."

Change is hard. Embracing change can be a challenging adjustment, but it can work if you are open. It can get lonely for a woman at times, but you can get your love from other people, not just a partner, such as friends, family, extended family, new connections and also, of course, your children. Be aware and respectful of your children's thoughts and feelings when you are finally ready to date, as eventually it could mean another person not only in your life but their lives also. By having a loving rapport with your kids, they won't see a new person as a threat. That bond you establish from early on cements your relationship with them, which will carry on into the future. Be gentle with yourself when re-entering the dating world after separation or divorce. The roller coaster that comes with it can be filled with highs and lows. Keep it in perspective and don't let it mean more than what it does. Don't let it define you. Don't overanalyse unsuccessful dates. Learn to open up and trust again, in your own time, and your self-empowerment will naturally build.

"Drink from the well of yourself and begin again."
– CHARLES BUKOWSKI

"New beginnings are often disguised as painful endings."
– LAO TZU

"Divorce never provides happiness, only the opportunity to find it and embrace it." –
CINDY HOLBROOK

"Who Said
Love Is Blind?
Always Look Fabulous."

Chapter 18
Love and Marriage

Do love and marriage really go together like a horse and carriage? Frank Sinatra seemed to think so. It does go together. It needs to be an ongoing investment in order for you to reap the benefits. Life and love is a gamble. Yet what happens if you don't take the risk? You may end up with nothing or you may have a life filled with wonderful adventures and fulfilment. Marriages are like stock market entities. You buy in with optimism and emotional highs, knowing what you want out of them and hoping that they can bring you all sorts of benefits and rewards. Emotional, spiritual, physical and mental rewards. You go through the ups and the downs. Sometimes there are some real downs. But like most investments, they are intended for the long term, not the short term. You weather the storms in order to reap the highs after the storms pass. You don't panic when there is a 'correction' in the market and all seems difficult and lost. You stick it out. You actually can come out better on the other side. Love can get tested many times in your life. Yet those who keep reinvesting together are the ones who can have something so profound that nothing can break them. All relationships are different. No two couples are the same. So what happens after the honeymoon? What happens after the 'I do' and the days of sweet bliss get lost in the everyday hustle and bustle of life?

"In the beginning it is great," says Tasmin, who's been married for ten years. "They want to impress you, they want your attention and adoration. Later down the track, men just get lazy and complacent. All the fuss, the gifts and random acts of kindness somehow get swept under the carpet. It's like they don't have to work hard anymore because they have you and they know you will be there regardless."

This sentiment rings true for many. It is natural that a relationship grows and evolves with time. But how does one 'date' in a relationship? How does a girl stay empowered when the relationship gets routine?

For most relationships, it's inevitable that the passion there in the beginning changes over time. But staying true to yourself, respecting your partnership and always having the lines of communication open is paramount. Keep the fire burning by being there for one another on a physical, mental, emotional and spiritual level.

"You are a team," Tasmin explains. "Make time for yourselves as a couple. Have a night out or cook something special. Plan a holiday. Buy tickets to a show. Do anything that gives you something to look forward to as a couple." Sometimes this allows both parties to connect on a different level and it's a good way to break up the monotony of everyday life. Making each other a priority is an empowering thing in itself.

We can become complacent without even knowing it. You can fall into everyday life and routine and time gets away from you so quickly. It is important to reconnect together on the same level. Make time for a nice dinner or long lunch, a bottle of wine or sunset-watching. It isn't always about gifts, it's about the thought process also – what you put into the idea behind a date or connection. It can be as simple and romantic as a handpicked flower left on the dresser, or a post-it note on the fridge that says, "I love you." It's not just the thought but the feelings it brings. A man could go the other way and give the 'grand gesture' of a gift. Perhaps a Chanel bag or a Hermes scarf. Grand gesture gifts go a long way for a woman. "Nothing says, 'You're my woman,' like a Chanel. You know you've made it when he comes home with a bag labelled Chanel," laughs Tasmin.

The focus should shift from the *what* to the *how*. Marriage is a long-term investment so it should always remain a top priority in your life if you expect it to succeed. Very often, it is the little things that count. The messages, the thought, the little gestures of love. One thought goes a long way. Mutual respect and consideration will serve you well, especially during challenging times. And we all have those.

So make time to date in marriage. It brings the fun back into the partnership and can remind you of the early days of intense passion. Keep reminding yourself of what attracted you to your spouse in the first place. Keep doing the things you love while also trying different things. Over time, successful marriages grow deeper. If you are with your best friend, then you are on the path of life together.

> *"Chains do not hold a marriage together. It is threads, hundreds of tiny threads which sew people together through the years."*
>
> – SIMONE SIGNORET

"The difference between an ordinary marriage and an extraordinary marriage is in giving just a little 'extra' every day, as often as possible, for as long as we both shall live."

— FAWN WEAVER

*"Looking To Another
For Your Self-Esteem
Will Eventually
Lead To Resentment."*

– TEYMARA ANTONIO WRIGHT

Chapter 19
Happy Ending

Empowerment stands for many things – emotions, strength, love, self-love, determination, growth, learning, happiness and so much more. No matter where you are in your life, the main concept is that regardless of your circumstances, you can always regain or retain your empowerment. Learn to train yourself to be strong and true to your inner spirit. No matter what age, demographic or chapter of life you're in, different challenges in your life will arise for various reasons. Even if it is difficult to comprehend or acknowledge at the time, it is part of life's plan.

We all have different opinions on what we want out of life and how we will choose to deal with situations. But your focus should be on encouraging and empowering yourself to be the best *you* can be. Make your emotional well-being your highest priority. This can be done by a shift in your awareness and focus. It is about being able to turn things around no matter what arises. Turn your attention inward, bring it all back to yourself and take control of your life before the negative patterns and feelings manifest into bigger problems. Rebuild one step at a time.

Whatever your 'label' – married, single, single with kids – try to tweak your perspective away from labelling yourself and instead see yourself as a capable human being. Focus on the moment and how you want to be and how you want to feel. Your current status isn't your lifelong status quo – particularly if you are not happy with it!

You can change it.

When you empower yourself, you can change anything. You are taking the reins and the responsibility. Being a woman in this day and age is a great privilege, as we have so many incredible examples of women before us who became leaders, role models and teachers. They paved the way for women today to gain a healthy control after setbacks and sadness. Women can work, earn, enjoy pleasures, and juggle families and work commitments. There is no better time on the planet to be a woman than now. Those before us have set the wheels in motion so we have the ability to empower each other to grow and achieve.

Don't let a label like 'married', 'divorced' or 'single' derail all the beauty that is within. Maintain the right perspective and the right attitude – even if it is your fifth bad date in a row and the right man is nowhere in sight. How do you do that? Be proud of you, even your flaws and past mistakes. Own them and be okay with them, for they shape you, not define you. When you look beyond, you will see something far greater – whether you have a ring on that finger or not. So no matter where you are in life, hold your head high and strut your stuff in those stilettos, girl! You've got this.

www.ingramcontent.com/pod-product-compliance
Lightning Source LLC
Chambersburg PA
CBHW051736020426
42333CB00014B/1345